The Breakdown
of Democratic Regimes

CRISIS, BREAKDOWN,
& REEQUILIBRATION

The Breakdown
of Democratic Regimes

CRISIS, BREAKDOWN, & REEQUILIBRATION

Juan J. Linz

The Johns Hopkins University Press

Baltimore and London

Originally published, 1978
Fourth printing, 1991

The Johns Hopkins University Press, 701 West 40th Street,
Baltimore, Maryland 21211
The Johns Hopkins Press Ltd., London

Library of Congress Cataloging in Publication Data

Linz Storch de Gracia, Juan José. 1926–
    The breakdown of democratic regimes; Crisis, Breakdown, and Reequilibration.

    Includes index.
    1.   Europe—Politics and government—20th century.
    2.   Latin America—Politics and government.   I.   Title
JN94.A2L56   320.9′4′05   78-571
ISBN 0-8018-2009-x pbk.

To Rocio

Contents

Editors' Preface and Acknowledgments

How and why democratic regimes break down are the central questions addressed by the contributors to this project.* Such breakdowns have long preoccupied social scientists. However, much of the existing literature on the subject has focused attention on the emergence of nondemocratic political forces or the underlying structural strains that lead to the collapse of democratic institutions.† Implicitly if not explicitly, the impression often given by such works is that of the virtual inevitability of the breakdown of the democratic regimes under discussion. While recognizing the scholarly legitimacy and analytic utility of studying antidemocratic movements and structural strains, we have addressed a somewhat different aspect of the breakdown of democratic regimes.

Given the tragic consequences of the breakdown of democracy in countries such as Germany, Spain, and Chile, we believed it intellectually and politically worthwhile to direct systematic attention to the dynamics of the political process of breakdown. In particular, we felt it important to analyze the behavior of those committed to democracy, especially the behavior of the incumbent democratic leaders, and to ask in what ways the actions or nonactions of the incumbents contributed to the breakdown under analysis. Did the prodemocratic forces have available to them other options that might have alleviated the crisis of democracy? Was the breakdown of democracy indeed inevitable? A closely related concern of the participants was the endeavor to abstract from the historical record recurrent patterns, sequences, and crises involved in the dynamic process of breakdown.

This publication has a long and complex history. Juan J. Linz's involvement with the question of the breakdown of democracy began with his concern with the fate of Spanish democracy, a fate that affected him as a child in Spain and as a citizen. Linz's reading of the monumental work on the breakdown of the Weimar Republic by Karl Dietrich Bracher led him to ask broad

---

*An extensive discussion of the definition of democracy and the criteria for the selection of cases is found in Juan Linz's volume, entitled *The Breakdown of Democratic Regimes: Crisis, Breakdown, and Reequilibration*. This volume appears as part 1 in the hardcover volume *The Breakdown of Democratic Regimes*. Parts 2, 3, and 4 examine the breakdown of democratic regimes in Europe, Latin America, and Chile.

†Much of this literature is discussed in the work by Linz just cited.

theoretical questions, which he explored with Daniel Bell at Columbia University in the mid-1960s. Linz and Alfred Stepan met at Columbia during this period, when Stepan was beginning to write a dissertation on the breakdown of democracy in Brazil, a process he had seen at first hand while writing articles in Latin America for the *Economist*. Other contributors who were at Columbia University at the same time included Paolo Farneti, Peter Smith, Arturo Valenzuela, and Alexander Wilde.

In order to encourage scholarly exchange on the political aspects of the breakdown of democracy, a panel was organized under the auspices of the Committee on Political Sociology, then under the chairmanship of S. M. Lipset. This panel met at a number of sessions at the Seventh World Congress of Sociology, held at Varna, Bulgaria, in 1970. Before the congress, Linz circulated a short paper titled "The Breakdown of Competitive Democracies: Elements for a Model," which became the focus of discussion by the members of the panel engaged in studies of individual countries and attending the congress. Among the contributors to the complete hardcover edition of this volume presenting initial drafts of the papers at Varna were Erik Allardt on Finland, Paolo Farneti on Italy, Rainer Lepsius on Weimar Germany, Juan Linz on Spain, Walter Simon on Austria, Peter Smith on Argentina, Alfred Stepan on Brazil, and Alexander Wilde on Colombia. Arend Lijphart was a stimulating commentator.*

After fruitful exchanges at Varna, we dispersed with the firm commitment to continue working on the project and to hold a conference in a few years focusing on the comparative and theoretical aspects of our work. In order to introduce other important cases and different perspectives Stepan encouraged Guillermo O'Donnell to write on the crisis of democracy in Argentina in the decade after the fall of Perón, and Julio Cotler and Daniel Levine to discuss the Peruvian and Venezuelan cases. After the overthrow of Allende in Chile, the editors invited Arturo Valenzuela to analyze the tragic events leading to the end of democracy in Chile.

With the generous support of the Concilium of International and Area Studies of Yale University, and the Joint Committee on Latin America of the Social Science Research Council and the American Council of Learned Societies, the augmented group met at Yale University in December 1973, at a conference chaired by Linz and Stepan, by then both members of the Yale faculty. At this meeting the papers presented benefited from the able suggestions of Douglas Chalmers, Edward Malefakis, and Eric Nordlinger, who acted as discussants. At the end of the conference the participants decided to

*The crisis of democracy in Portugal in the 1920s, France in the 1950s, Peru and Greece in the 1960s, and the continuing conflict in Northern Ireland were also discussed in papers presented by Herminio Martins, Steven Cohn, David Chaplin, Charles Moskos, and Richard Rose, respectively. Conflicting obligations did not permit them to continue with the project. Richard Rose developed his paper in a somewhat different direction and published it separately as a book, *Governing without Consensus: An Irish Perspective* (Boston: Beacon Press, 1971).

revise their work in the light of one another's findings and the collective discussion of areas of similarity and dissimilarity. A year at the Institute for Advanced Study in Princeton supported by a grant from the National Science Foundation to the Institute allowed Linz to revise his introduction and maintain contact with the co-authors.

Despite the group's interest in underlying, recurrent patterns of breakdown, there has been no attempt to force individual contributors into the procrustean bed of the editors' own thinking. The reader will discover important differences in the authors' intellectual orientations, which grew in part out of the diversity of the democracies studied and reflect in part genuine differences of opinion on the relative weight to be attached to political forces, even after these forces had been given due consideration by all contributors.

It should be stressed that this volume is an initial social scientific effort at middle-level generalizations about complex historical reality. Such a work is, of course, never a substitute for fundamental historical studies of individual cases; rather, it builds upon such studies and, we hope, draws the attention of historians to more generalized propositions, propositions they can in turn pursue further in their own work. Although we are concerned with middle-level generalizations, it is the editors' view that the historicity of macro-political processes precludes the highly abstract generalizing of ahistorical social scientific models of the type susceptible to computer simulations and applicable to all past and any future cases. It is our hope, nevertheless, that scholars interested in developing more formal models may build on our work and incorporate into their models the complex realities here discussed. At this stage of the analysis our collective attention to the political dynamics of the breakdown of democracies has brought to light a number of recurring elements which are discussed at length in Linz's introductory essay. The independent contributions made to breakdowns by political incumbents is a theme that emerges in almost all the papers and has justified our attention to this aspect of the problem, an aspect all too often overlooked.

The individual studies shed new light on some of the most historically important cases of breakdown of democracy, such as Germany, Italy, Spain, and Chile. In addition, some of the less well-known cases forcefully illustrate hitherto neglected aspects of the question of the survival of democracy. Daniel Levine's study of Venezuela examines a fascinating case of political learning. Ten years after the breakdown in Venezuela in 1948, many of the institutional participants in the breakdown—the church, the army, the political parties—consciously and successfully devised strategies to avoid such a breakdown when a new attempt to forge democratic institutions began in 1958. Alexander Wilde's discussion of the reequilibration of Colombian democracy in the 1950s also shows how political learning was crucial for the construction of a consociational democracy. The chapter by Risto Alapuro and Erik Allardt discusses the little-known case of Finland, in which, despite intense conflict, the process of breakdown described in other chapters was avoided. The analysis of nonoccurrence as well as of occurrence increased our understanding of the breakdown process.

With the publication of this project, many of the contributors are turning their attention to closely related issues that loom large on the scholarly agenda. High priority for further work along these lines should now be given to the analysis of the conditions that lead to the breakdown of authoritarian regimes, to the process of transition from authoritarian to democratic regimes, and especially to the political dynamics of the consolidation of postauthoritarian democracies.

The editors want to thank The Johns Hopkins University Press for its help in publishing a project of such large intellectual scope and sheer physical size as this one. We want to give special thanks to Henry Y. K. Tom, the social sciences editor of the Press, for his great assistance. The project would not have arrived in the reader's hands without extensive copy editing. Jean Savage and Victoria Suddard helped in the early stages of copy editing.

Yale University

JUAN J. LINZ
ALFRED STEPAN

The Breakdown
of Democratic Regimes

CRISIS, BREAKDOWN, & REEQUILIBRATION

1.

Introduction

A change of political regime affects millions of lives, stirring a spectrum of emotions from fear to hope. The March on Rome, the *Machtergreifung* by Hitler, the Spanish civil war, Prague in February of 1948, the coup against Allende—such dramas, symbolizing the transfer of power, become fixed in the memory of people as pivotal dates in their lives. Yet the events themselves are in truth the culmination of a longer process, an incremental political change that has evolved over a more or less prolonged period. Is there a common pattern in the processes that have led to changes of regime, or is each a unique historical situation? Is it possible to construct a descriptive model of the process of the breakdown of democracy that could ultimately contribute to a better understanding of its elements and dynamics? If it were possible to construct such a model, which would be an explanatory model, would we know more about the conditions for stability of democracy?

Certainly the problem of the stability and overthrow of political systems has long occupied the minds of those who study politics. In recent years social scientists have devoted considerable attention to the study of the prerequisites for political stability, particularly in democracies.[1] Analyses, however, have tended to be static, with more emphasis on the social, economic, and cultural correlates of stable regimes in a given moment of time than on the dynamic processes of crisis, breakdown, and reequilibration of existing regimes or the consolidation of new ones. This emphasis has resulted primarily from the availability of systematic and quantitative data on a large number of polities and of new techniques in statistical analysis.[2] It has also reflected postwar optimism about the durability of democracies, once established. At the same time, however, historians have provided detailed records of the events and the social, economic, and political changes leading to those dramatic moments that brought Mussolini, Hitler, and Franco to power or, as in France, led to a turnabout in the battle of a democracy to survive. Further perspectives on events and situations are available to us in the wealth of personal writings by those who helped shape history.[3]

It would seem fruitful, therefore, to combine the knowledge of the events themselves, derived from the accounts of historians and the records of participants, with the problem formulations derived from contemporary social sci-

4   JUAN J. LINZ

ence in our effort to construct a descriptive model—and perhaps ultimately an explanatory model—of the processes operating in a change of regime.[4] Analysis of many seemingly unique historical situations suggests the possibility of common patterns—certain sequences of events that recur in country after country. In fact, the participants often seem aware of such chains of events, and express such awareness in widespread attitudes of resignation, tragedy, inevitability, or hubris.[5]

In these analyses, social scientists, particularly sociologists (especially those with a Marxist orientation), tend to emphasize the structural characteristics of societies—socioeconomic infrastructures that act as a constraining condition, limiting the choices of political actors. They focus on the underlying social conflicts, particularly class conflicts, that in their view make the stability of liberal democratic institutions unlikely, if not impossible. They contend that breakdown is sufficiently explained by great social and economic inequity, concentration of economic power, economic dependency on other countries, and the inevitable antidemocratic reaction of the privileged against the institutions that allow the mobilization of the masses against the existing socioeconomic order. We would be the last to deny the importance of those factors and their considerable effect in particular cases.[6] Yet even if sociological analyses or those based on culture, national character, or psychological variables could explain *why* the breakdown occurs, we still would have to ask *how*.

In our view, one cannot ignore the actions of either those who are more or less interested in the maintenance of an open democratic political system or those who, placing other values higher, are unwilling to defend it or even ready to overthrow it. These are the actions that constitute the true dynamics of the political process.[7] We feel that the structural characteristics of societies—their actual and latent conflicts—constitute a series of opportunities and constraints for the social and political actors, both men and institutions, that can lead to one or another outcome. We shall start from the assumption that those actors have certain choices that can increase or decrease the probability of the persistence and stability of a regime.[8] Undoubtedly, the resulting actions or events tend to have a cumulative and reinforcing effect that increases or decreases the probability of survival of democratic politics. Certainly, in the last stages before the denouement, the opportunities to save the system might be minimal. Our model, therefore, will be probabilistic rather than deterministic.

In this context, the analysis of cases in which a democracy in crisis managed to reequilibrate becomes particularly interesting, since it would prove *a contrario* some of the hypotheses we shall develop. The special merit of Karl Dietrich Bracher's brilliant description of the fall of the Weimar Republic was his emphasis on the patterned and sequential character of the breakdown process through the phases of loss of power, power vacuum, and takeover of power.[9] We shall focus on those more strictly political variables that tend to be neglected in many other approaches to the problem of stable democracy, because in our view political processes actually precipitate the ultimate breakdown.[10] We shall do so without ignoring the basic social, economic, and cultural conditioning variables. It also would seem that without attention to the historical political process, it would be difficult to explain why political institutions in different societies do not suffer the same fate on experiencing similar strains. In crisis situations like those we shall be discussing, leadership, even the presence of an individual with unique qualities and characteristics—a Charles de Gaulle, for instance—can be decisive and cannot be predicted by any model.[11] Even so, we hope to show that certain types of individual and institutional actors confronted with similar situations have a high probability of responding in ways that contribute to the breakdown of regimes. It is our task to describe and, as far as possible, account for those actions on the road toward breakdown or reequilibration of democracies.

We do not hesitate to admit that our problem formulation seeks to point out opportunities that democratic leaders might use to assure the consolidation, stability, persistence, and reequilibration of their regimes, as well as the pitfalls likely to be encountered in the process. We would hope that our knowledge will help them in their efforts, even though our insights, if valid, should also be useful to those who want to attend a "school for dictators."[12]

Breakdown of Competitive Democracies

The focus of our analysis and of the essays in this book is on competitive democracies,[13] with no attempt here to extend the study to authoritarian, totalitarian, or traditional political systems.[14]

To avoid any misunderstanding of our intellectual effort, it is necessary to define with some precision the type of regime whose breakdown we are analyzing. Our criteria for a democracy may be summarized as follows: legal freedom to formulate and advocate political alternatives with the concomitant rights to free association, free speech, and other basic freedoms of person; free and nonviolent competition among leaders with periodic validation of their claim to rule; inclusion of all effective political offices in the democratic process; and provision for the participation of all members of the political community, whatever their political preferences. Practically, this means the freedom to create political parties and to conduct free and honest elections at regular intervals without excluding any effective political office from direct or indirect electoral accountability. Today "democracy" implies at least universal male suffrage, but perhaps in the past it would extend to the regimes with property, taxation, occupational, or literacy requirements of an earlier period, which limited suffrage to certain social groups.

The exclusion from political competition of parties not committed to the legal pursuit of power—which in reality is limited to enforceable exclusions (of minor parties or of individuals on a temporal and partial basis, as in political screening for civil service)—is not incompatible with the guarantee of free competition in our definition of a democracy.[15] It is the legal equal opportunity for the expression of all opinions and protection by the state against arbitrary and above all, violent interference with that right, rather than an unconditional opportunity for the expression of opinions, that distinguishes a democratic regime. Our definition of democracy would not include regimes that might once have received the genuine support of a majority but have since become unwilling to submit their power to revalidation by the society. It does not require a turnover of parties in power, but the possibility of such a turnover, even when such alternation is prima facie evidence of the democratic character of a regime.[16]

There can be no doubt that social and political realities in countries included in our analysis have sometimes led them to deviate from even our minimal definition. This is particularly true for the Latin American states and also for rural Italy south of Rome during the first decades of the century, when administrative, social, and economic pressures imposed limits on political civil liberties to the point that even the counting of ballots was suspect. Deviation from the democratic ideal does not necessarily constitute its denial, however, and the regimes under consideration all satisfied our minimal criteria. Only the inclusion of Peru and Colombia might be questioned. That few additional countries—notably Japan in the interwar years, Czechoslovakia, Latvia, Lithuania, perhaps some Balkan countries, and Greece after World War II—might have been included in our analysis indicates how small a number of democracies qualifies even under our minimal definition.

We have deliberately omitted from our definition any reference to the prevalence of democratic values, social relations, equality of opportunities in the occupational world, and education, as our focus here is the breakdown of political democracy, not crisis in democratic societies. The influence of political democracy on nonpolitical aspects of a society—or conversely, the effect of a nondemocratic culture on the persistence or failure of a democratic regime—is clearly worth studying; to include in our definition, however, such elements as the democratization of the society and the degree of equality would not ônly prevent us from asking many relevant questions but would reduce the number of cases in our analysis.

Given this definition, neither the transformation of a postdemocratic into a totalitarian system, the internal changes leading to posttotalitarian regimes (as in the de-Stalinization of Communist regimes), the breakdown of authoritarian regimes (Portugal in 1974), nor the transition to democracy of traditional monarchical rule fall within our purview. No doubt there are processes common to the breakdown of any regime, and processes distinctive to the fall of democracies, but it would be difficult, without a comparative study of regime changes in both democratic and nondemocratic systems, to isolate the variables and identify them as one or the other. This is not to overlook some general patterns. No system that could be called totalitarian in any meaningful sense of the term has broken down through internal causes, even those systems that have experienced sufficient transformation to be described as post-totalitarian authoritarian regimes.[17] The Nazi system, and even Fascist rule in Italy—which might be considered an arrested totalitarianism—were overthrown only by external defeat. The breakdown of most authoritarian regimes has led not to the establishment of democracy but to the estalishment of another authoritarian regime—perhaps in the case of Cuba, a totalitarian system—after a coup or a revolution. Study of the few cases in which an authoritarian regime transformed itself into a democracy, or was overthrown to give place to one, could contribute to our understanding of the common variables. Although that number is small, there are several cases in which democracies were succeeded by authoritarian regimes and in turn by the reestablishment of democracy. The contributors to this volume who deal with such cases have used the opportunity to explore how one fatal crisis of democracy helped later democratic rulers to avoid some of the errors of their predecessors.[18]

We have not included a number of postcolonial democracies that had little time to become institutionalized, whose form of government was largely a transplant from the mother country, and whose consolidation of political institutions usually coincided with the process of state-building. We doubt that our analysis would be applicable to the breakdown of postindependence democratic institutions in Africa and Asia, as in Nigeria or Pakistan, for it is limited in almost every case to states whose existence was consolidated before they became democracies. (Only Finland acquired statehood after World War I, and Austria emerged as a separate state out of the Austrian-Hungarian Empire by the *diktat* of the victors.)

The democracies to which our model applies are all nation-states, even Spain, which, though it has a multinational character for some Spaniards, is regarded by most as a nation-state. Only in Austria, where a significant number of citizens identified with Germany, was the existence of the nation-state questioned. Undoubtedly, including Czechoslovakia in the interwar years and a multinational country like Yugoslavia in our analysis would have highlighted the importance of cultural and linguistic conflicts in the crisis of democracy—though in the case of Czechoslovakia it would be difficult to isolate the internal strains from the external pressures that led to Munich and the secession of Slovakia, and subsequently the end of democracy and independence as well.[19]

Should the regimes on which our analysis is based properly be considered competitive democracies, or should they be classified as a special type of democratic regime? The chapters on some of the Latin American countries will quickly establish characteristics in their democratic institutions, especially in operational aspects, that differentiate them from the old established democracies of Western Europe and even from the unstable "democracies in the making" of Europe. In fact, Alexander Wilde suggested that we should use a modified and less demanding definition of democracy in terms of some common characteristics of competitive political institutions and the peculiar forms that those institutions might take. Unfortunately, there is no meaningful, accepted typology of competitive democracies, nor any accepted measure of the degree of democracy. Only the distinction between democracies based on majority rule and those that Lijphart calls "consociational" has gained wide acceptance.[20] Our analysis includes no democracies that could properly be classified as consociational; in fact, none of those so characterized has experienced a breakdown of its institutions. This leads us to suspect that the very political mechanisms described by the term "consociational democracy" might be very effective in handling the strains that might otherwise endanger their democratic institutions. Certainly, the democracies normally considered consociational—the Netherlands, Belgium, Switzerland, post–World War II Austria, and, until its recent breakdown, Lebanon—share many other characteristics favorable to democratic stability.

In summary, our analysis is applicable only to democratic regimes in consolidated nation-states that had achieved independence or a measure of political autonomy a considerable time before the crisis of the regime. In addition, all the democracies analyzed are based on majority rule rather than on complex consociational mechanisms.

Stillborn or Embattled New Democracies

The question of whether our model of the breakdown process might not be based on regimes established only shortly before the crisis that triggered their downfall, and that we might, therefore, be dealing with a failure of consolidation rather than the breakdown of a democratic regime, is an important one.[21] Such a model, it could be argued, would not be applicable to regimes satisfying the requirement of persistence of patterns elaborated by Harry Eckstein, and particularly not to those that had enjoyed a stable existence of a more than one generation, like the United Kingdom, Switzerland, the Scandinavian countries, Belgium, the Netherlands, and even France.[22]

This point cannot be ignored, and we shall return to it when we emphasize the importance of the belief in the legitimacy of democratic institutions as a factor increasing the likelihood of stability in a democracy. Undoubtedly, stability breeds stability, to put it tautologically. Old democracies were once new, beset by the risks facing all new democracies, even in those cases in which it could be argued that the historical evolution was slower and more involved with continuity of traditional institutions and elites, thus confronting rulers with fewer and more manageable problems. Furthermore, some of the older democracies had the advantage of being small and relatively prosperous countries—those in certain parts of Europe, for example.[23] Historians and sociologists have drawn attention to the unique circumstances under which the transformation of traditional political systems into modern democracies took place in such cases. It could be argued that whenever those slow and unique developments leading to democracy were absent, even before the French Revolution, the probability for the consolidation of democracy was considerably lower.

However, while the specific regimes that were overthrown in such countries as Portugal, Germany, Austria, and Spain had only recently been established, liberal democratic processes had in each case gained ascendancy over half a century, if not longer, under constitutional or semiconstitutional monarchies. In Italy the constitutional monarchy had been instituted simultaneously with the building of the nation in the Risorgimento and had undergone a process of democratization that accelerated, along with that of many more stable democracies, in the first decades of the century, particularly after World War I. In spite of deviations from the ideal represented by oligarchy, limited democracy, and authoritarian periods, the Latin American countries were strongly committed ideologically to liberal democracy, and no other legitimacy formula had wide appeal. It is true that a number of countries had significant intellectual minorities that defended other political formulas, but large majorities favored a legal, rational, democratic legitimacy formula. Only in Germany did the conservative antidemocratic ideologies gain wide and organized acceptance in important sectors of society before the breakthrough of democracy in 1918.

In summary, in the countries analyzed here democracy per se was not new, nor did it in most cases have to contend with widespread hostility before the onset of the crisis, though certain specific regimes and the regime-building forces established only a few years before their demise did come under such attack. It could be argued that in many cases the attack was not initially directed against democracy itself but against the particular content that the regime-building and sustaining forces wanted to give it. In fact, willingness to offer those favoring a different political and social order a more effective role and some guarantees within the democratic process might have prevented their disaffection. Obviously, it is not always possible to distinguish the form of democracy from its substantive content. What is initially conceived as an attack on particular governing forces, therefore, turns quickly into an overthrow of democratic institutions by force or manipulation that makes reestablishment of such institutions impossible for almost a generation.

A somewhat different but related question is raised by those who contend that the democracies that failed or were overthrown had been instaured under conditions that made their success extremely unlikely. To put it more graphically, they were stillborn. Certainly historians can argue that the circumstances surrounding the birth of a new regime—the underlying social structure, the latent social conflicts, and the institutional and ideological heritage from previous regimes—were such that, unless the new democratic rulers were able in an initial phase to transform the society, any serious crisis would inevitably have a destructive outcome. This point of view has often been argued in connection with the Weimar Republic and can be sustained with even more cogency in many Latin American cases.[24] In fact, the theorists of the *dependencia* tend to consider the solution of social problems the prerequisite of a stable regime. On a broad historical scale, Barrington Moore has advanced the thesis that unless societies have experienced a basic socioeconomic revolution, particularly in the agrarian power relations and the economic systems associated with the great political revolutions of the West, democracy has no chance of survival.[25]

Without ignoring the insights that can be derived from these approaches, we contend that a large part of the breakdown process cannot be accounted for by those variables. Indeed, there are countries whose democracies have enjoyed considerable periods of stability in spite of those identical initial handicaps.[26] Therefore, we would not say that such democracies were stillborn, even granting that some may have had genetic defects or an aborted period of consolidation. Precedent conditions may, as we shall see, limit the capacity of a regime to handle crises, but breakdown itself cannot be explained without paying attention to political processes taking place after its instauration. The elements favorable to democracy under precedent authoritarian or semidemocratic constitutional regimes, the discrediting and failure of the predemocratic regimes, and the enthusiasm and hope created by the new regimes should not be underestimated. No regime enjoys the full support or compliance of all of its citizens. According to Richard Rose's typology of regime authority, few regimes are fully legitimate or coercive, and most function in a range of intermediate categories.[27] The question is, then, what causes a regime to move beyond its functional range to become a disrupted or semicoercive regime that ends in repudiation by large or critical segments of the population?

To phrase the question otherwise would be to say that only democracies enjoying high support and high compliance over long periods of time have a significant chance of avoiding breakdown and repudiation, a hypothesis that would be almost tautological, in addition to being unduly pessimistic. Our hypothesis is that the democratic regimes under study had at one point or another a reasonable chance to survive and become fully consolidated, but that certain characteristics and actions of relevant actors—institutions as well as individuals—decreased the probability of such a development. Our analysis makes the assumption that those actions show a pattern repeated with variations in a number of societies. The repetition of the same or similar patterns in the breakdown process might give rise to a deterministic interpretation. We want to emphasize, however, the probabilistic character of our analysis and to stress that at any point in the process up to the final point chances remain, albeit diminishing chances, to save the regime. One is reminded of the great German historian Meinecke's comment, upon hearing the news of Hitler's appointment as chancellor: "This was not necessary."[28] It would be tempting to try to define at each juncture and for each regime what the odds were in favor of its survival, but our guess is that even after the most painstaking comparative research, few scholars would agree on the probability to be assigned to each case.

Socioeconomic Change as a Factor

Another assumption of our analysis that is open to question is that the distinctive political processes common to competitive democracies are valued in and of themselves by significant sectors of society. The contrary assumption is that democratic institutions are valued only insofar as they produce policies satisfactory to their supporters. Put another way, allegiance to any political system exists only insofar as it guarantees the persistence of, or the opportunity to change, a certain social, normally socioeconomic, order. According to that view, democracy is only a means to an end. Once people realize that their goals cannot be achieved through democratic institutions, the democratic system will be discarded. Those taking this position generally have in mind a certain socioeconomic order, but the same sequence could be postulated for a cultural, religious, or international order.

Obviously, these are extreme formulations of two positions that do not correspond to any concrete historical reality. While legal, rational, democratic authority in the Weberian sense in theory demands allegiance irrespective of the content that the democratic political process would give it,[29] both the "natural law" tradition and the more sociological Schumpeterian analysis underline the fact that no democracy can be based exclusively on such an abstract claim of legitimacy.[30] Yet we also decidedly reject the assumption that any type of regime is simply the expression and defense of a particular socioeconomic, cultural, or religious order. In fact, democracy is the type of political institutionalization that allows change in those orders without immediate changes in the political sphere, as well as permitting considerable independent influence by the political leadership on those other sectors of the social order. Certainly, *hinc et nunc* and in the short run, it is only analytically possible to separate the political regime from a given social order or from particular processes of politically imposed change. In a longer time perspective, democracy can serve many and changing ends, and can defend and contribute to the creation of different social and economic orders. Therefore, in principle, a democratic system should be able to rally legions of people pursuing widely varying goals over time. Only in the short run and with a zero-sum, either/or view of conflicts in society—both stances characteristic of extremist positions—does support for democracy as distinct from support for a particular conception of the social order become impossible and meaningless.

Extremist politics are the result of structural strains, and in certain societies, in certain historical situations, they engage large segments of the population. However, their capacity to do so is generally a reflection of a failure of the democratic leadership. The democratic system itself is not the generator. In our view, a democracy is unlikely to be supported unconditionally, irrespective of policies and outcomes for different social groups, but neither is it supported or challenged just because of its identification with a particular social, specifically socioeconomic, order.[31] Analytically, four different situations can be distinguished, depending on the degree of legitimacy granted by majorities of the population to the democratic political institutions and to the socioeconomic system they defend or are in the process of creating. Certainly, the ideal situation occurs when very large majorities grant legitimacy to both political institutions and the socioeconomic system, and when the social order is not perceived as unjust nor is reasonable change seen as threatening to those who enjoy a privileged position in the existing order. When both are considered illegitimate, little stability can be expected either of the regime or of the society, except through use of large-scale coercion. Most societies that have experienced changes of regime have fallen in the two intermediary situations in the typology, when one's or the other's loss of legitimacy obtains. In those cases a complex set of interrelationships and feedbacks exists between the political and social systems.

To say precisely how much the hostility to, or rigid defense of, the social order contributed to the crisis of the political system, and how much the weakening or loss of legitimacy of the political order exacerbated economic and social problems, would be difficult and would have to be determined in each particular case. For our theoretical purposes, however, it is important to emphasize that the two processes can be kept analytically distinct, though in reality both are likely to occur.[32] Making these assumptions, our political analysis of the historical process of breakdown might have greater or lesser relevance to each, but in neither case would it be irrelevant. The constraints imposed on significant segments of society by the illegitimacy of the existing social order or the changes it is undergoing will affect the degree of freedom to institutionalize and defend democratic political institutions, perhaps limiting—though never obliterating—the range of choice for the political actors. In fact, in those situations the consolidation of legitimate political institutions becomes more important in assuring continued, slow, but nonviolent social change. Rapid revolutionary social change in such circumstances is probably incompatible with democracy; as both radicals and conservatives might agree, the option is one or the other, whether explicitly or implicitly. It is no accident that political actors who are highly indignant about the injustice of the social order are often ready to risk the stability of democracy, which for them is a lesser value than social change. This is the source of the ambivalence of many Socialists, particularly Marxists, toward political democracy.[33] The resultant ambivalent and indecisive policies of their leaders have been a major factor in the breakdown of democracy in many countries—Italy, Austria, Spain, Chile, and to a lesser extent, Germany. The radical critic of the existing social order or, for that matter, of the cultural or religious order, might maintain that if in the short run democracy cannot serve as an instrument for decisive social change, it does not deserve his loyalty. What he might not realize is that the alternative is not revolutionary change, imposed in authoritarian fashion, but the reversal of slow processes of change under conditions of freedom and compromise, by counterrevolutionary authoritarian rule.

Analysis focused largely on actions by democratic rulers that increase or decrease the probability of a breakdown is not unrelated to the assumption that such leaders, at least in the short run, should value the persistence of democratic institutions as highly if not more highly than other goals. Not everyone will (or should) agree with that assumption, but irrespective of such agreement, we feel that it is intellectually legitimate to study the problem of breakdown from this perspective.[34]

2.
Elements of Breakdown

Revolution and Regime Breakdowns

⟨ Those who accede to power after the breakdown of a democracy often speak of their "revolution," thereby claiming for themselves the aura of legitimacy attached to that word and what it symbolizes. Most of these so-called revolutions, however, have been military coups d'état or semi- or pseudo-legal transfers of power rather than violent takeovers: *Machtübernahme* rather than *Machtergreifung*.[1] There are exceptions, however; in Spain, the civil war of 1936–39 bears closer resemblance to the aftermath of the fall of the czarist regime, traditional rule in China, or colonial rule in Vietnam and other Third World countries. If the term "revolution" is used in another sense—radical change of the social structure—it cannot be applied, since most of the breakdowns have been counterrevolutionary, in that they have aimed at preventing radical changes in the social structure, even though they often culminated in decisive changes. "Revolution" in the more restrictive sense of association with changes guided by leftist ideologies is inapplicable as well, since none of the relatively stabilized democracies has fallen under the onslaught of the left, although revolutionary attempts by the Left, or more often just the talk of revolution, contributed decisively to the crisis and breakdown of democracy in Italy, Spain, Chile, and to a lesser extent, Germany.⟩ The success of the great revolutions in the twentieth century against traditional, authoritarian, and colonial regimes owes much to the disorganization and the delegitimation of the so-called Establishment due to external wars and defeat.[2] Probably only the ultimate changes after the breakdown of German democracy in 1933 and the subsequent totalitarian transformation of society under the Nazis can in some sense of the word be called revolutionary.[3] The Spanish revolution of the Left that was initiated after the military uprising against the Republic was finally defeated by counter-revolutionary forces. ⟨Thus, despite some overlap between breakdown of democratic regimes and revolutions, the two phenomena can and must be studied separately, lest we stretch the concept of revolution beyond recognition.⟩

As we shall see, political violence is both an important indicator and a contributing cause of breakdown, but the line between cause and effect is blurred. In a number of cases in the present study, the amount of politically

14

significant violence was relatively minor, even when a distorted perception of that violence and a low threshold of tolerance for violence in the society contributed to the breakdown. Undoubtedly, the study of political and social violence is central to our problem, but the theories advanced to explain the amount and character of violence are not sufficient to account for the breakdown of regimes and will be treated as explanations of one of the contributing factors.[4] Research on the beginnings, patterns, and causes of collective and individual violence in democracies in crisis is needed, but the need is even greater for research on the contemporary perception of that violence and the responses of different elites to it. The techniques of collective history developed by French historians should be applied to the study of these elites, particularly the activists on the right, who often are neglected in such analyses.[5]

In the past, when democratic regimes had acquired a certain stability they could be threatened by challengers, who would persuade important sectors of the population to switch allegiance from government to challenger. They would then undermine the regime's authority by demonstrating its inability to maintain order, forcing it to resort to an unwarranted, arbitrary, and indiscriminate use of power that often led to further withdrawal of support. In modern societies, however, governments faced with such threats can generally count on the compliance of many citizens, their staff, bureaucrats, policemen, and the military if they decide to activate their commitments to legitimate authority. Therefore, disloyal oppositions have tended increasingly to avoid direct confrontation with governments and their agents and have aimed instead at combining their illegal actions with a formally legal process of transfer of power. In that process the neutrality, if not the cooperation, of the armed forces or a sector of them has become decisive. The twentieth century has seen fewer revolutions started by the populace than the nineteenth, and their fate in modern states has generally been defeat. The Communists and Nazis learned that lesson. Mussolini's combination of illegal action and legal takeover became the new model for overthrow of democracies.[6] Only the direct intervention of the military seems to be able to topple regimes in modern stabilized states. This probably explains why, despite the revolutionary mobilization of the masses by leftist parties and their partial successes, none of the democracies whose breakdown we can study was toppled by a revolution or takeover by the parties of the Left. The Czechoslovakia of 1948 was the only democracy taken over by the Communists, but in that case it is difficult to separate the internal processes that have some similarity to the breakdowns we shall study from the presence of the Soviet army and the influence of the Soviet Union.[7] The outcome of the breakdown of democratic regimes generally seems to be the victory of political forces identified as rightists, even when that term might not exactly describe their policies in power. This does not mean that in many cases the Left did not play a decisive role in weakening democratic governments and provoking their overthrow.

Legitimacy, Efficacy, Effectiveness, and the Breakdown of Democracy

Our analysis starts with the existence of a government that has attained its power through a democratic process of free elections and claims the obedience of the citizens within its territory on that basis, with a relatively high probability that they will comply. That obedience may spring from a wide range of motives, from fear of the sanctions that could be imposed to positive support based on the belief in the government's right to demand obedience.[8] Most people, of course, obey out of habit and rational calculation of advantage. In principle, however, democratic regimes are based on much more. More than any other type of regime, they depend for support on the activation of commitments for the implementation of decisions binding on the collectivity. In normal times, habit and rational calculation of advantage might assure compliance, but in crisis situations, when the authority of the government is challenged by some group in the society, or when decisions affect many citizens negatively, this is not sufficient. It becomes even less so when those in authority must make use of force, asking others to risk their lives and to take the lives of fellow citizens in the defense of the political order.

Weber formulated it as follows: "Custom, personal advantage, purely affectual or ideal motives of solidarity do not form a sufficiently reliable basis for a given domination. In addition there is normally a further element, the belief in *legitimacy*."[9] In the words of a democratic political leader: " . . . the most effective means of upholding the law is not the state policemen or the marshals or the national guard. It is you. It lies in your courage to accept those laws with which you disagree as well as those with which you agree."[10] This belief in legitimacy assures the capacity of a government to enforce decisions. Obviously no government is accorded legitimacy in this sense by all its citizens, but no government can survive without that belief on the part of a substantial number of citizens and an even larger number of those in control of the armed forces. Democratic governments require that belief, with more or less intensity, at least within the ranks of the majority. Normally a democratic government should enjoy that legitimacy even among those who constitute its opposition. This is what is meant by the expression "loyal" opposition. At the very least, legitimacy is the belief that in spite of shortcomings and failures, the existing political institutions are better than any others that might be established, and that they therefore can demand obedience. Ultimately it means that when the rulers who hold power constitutionally demand obedience, and another group questions that demand in the name of alternative political arrangements, citizens will voluntarily opt for compliance with the demands of those in authority. More specifically, the legitimacy of a democratic regime rests on the belief in the right of those legally elevated to authority to issue certain types of commands, to expect obedience, and to enforce them, if necessary, by the use of force. "In a democracy, citizens are free to disagree with the law, but not to disobey it, for in a government of laws, and not of men, no one, however prominent or powerful, and no mob, however unruly or boisterous, is entitled to defy them."[11] That belief does not require agreement with the content of the norm or support for a particular government, but it does require acceptance of its binding character and its right to issue commands until changed by the procedures of the regime. In democracies such change implies gaining control of the government without the use of force, according to constitutional procedures such as free competition for the peaceful support of the majority of citizens, legitimate forms of influence, and the use of constitutional mechanisms to control the decisions of the rulers. That belief is based on the expectation that the rulers, if challenged and required to abandon power by legitimate means, will not attempt to retain power by illegitimate means. Democratic legitimacy, therefore, requires adherence to the rules of the game by both a majority of the voting citizens and those in positions of authority, as well as trust on the part of the citizenry in the government's commitment to uphold them.

In every society, there are those who deny legitimacy to any government and those who believe in alternative legitimacy formulae.[12] Regimes vary widely in the amount and intensity of citizen belief in their legitimacy. In the case of a democracy, however, belief in its legitimacy by a majority of the population or even a majority of the electorate is insufficient for stability. Belief in that legitimacy on the part of those who have direct control of armed forces is particularly important. However, it seems unlikely that military leaders would turn their arms against the government unless they felt that a significant segment of the society shared their lack of belief and that others were at least indifferent to the conflicting claims for allegiance.[13]

Legitimacy is granted or withdrawn by each member of the society day in and day out. It does not exist outside the actions and attitudes of individuals. Regimes therefore enjoy more or less legitimacy just by existing. Gains and losses of support for governments, leaders, parties, and policies in a democracy are likely to fluctuate rapidly while the belief in the legitimacy of the system persists. There is clearly an interaction between the support for the regime and that for the governing parties, which in the absence of other indicators leads to the use of electoral returns and public opinion responses as indirect evidence of the legitimacy of the system. Consequently, the loss of support for all political actors in a democratic regime is likely to lead to an erosion of legitimacy, just as widespread support for a government, particu-

[Handwritten margin notes:] Belief in the legitimacy of those who control of armed forces imp. However, it seems unlikely that Military leaders would turn their arms against the govt unless they felt a signif. segment of the society shared their feeling + that others were at least indifferent.

larly beyond those supporting it with their votes, is likely to contribute to the strength of legitimacy.[14]

Why do people believe in the legitimacy of democratic institutions? Answering this question is almost as difficult as explaining why people believe in particular religious dogmas, for, as is the case with religious beliefs, the degree of understanding, of skepticism and faith, varies widely across the society and over time.[15] Undoubtedly, political socialization plays a decisive role, and this is an advantage for long-established democratic regimes whose educational system, mass media, and high culture have made democratic ideals pervasive and understandable. As in the case of other social beliefs, the major role in formulating, elaborating, and transmitting the legitimacy formulae is played by the intellectuals. There is also what the Germans would call a *Zeitgeist,* a feeling shared across national boundaries, that a particular type of political system is the most desirable or the most questionable. This feeling tends to be reinforced or weakened by the positive or negative perception of other more powerful states or nations that are successful with a particular type of regime. In the interwar years the *Zeitgeist* was deeply affected by the success of Fascist Italy, and later Nazism, and this helped weaken the commitment to democratic legitimacy in many countries. As Weber noted, no type of legitimacy is found in pure form in any society. Most people give allegiance to a regime on the basis of a complex set of beliefs. Democratic legitimacy, therefore, is often reinforced by becoming a form of tradition, and the personal charisma of democratic leaders committed to the regime tends to reinforce its institutions.[16]

Our minimal definition of legitimacy, then, is a relative one: a legitimate government is one considered to be the least evil of the forms of government. Ultimately, democratic legitimacy is based on the belief that for that particular country at that particular historical juncture no other type of regime could assure a more successful pursuit of collective goals.[17]

At this point two other dimensions characterizing a political system become relevant—its efficacy and its effectiveness.[18] In the course of time both can strengthen, reinforce, maintain, or weaken the belief in legitimacy. However, the relationships between these variables are far from fully transitive and lineal, since perception of the efficacy and effectiveness of a regime tends to be biased by the initial commitments to its legitimacy. Legitimacy, at least for a time, operates as a positive constant that multiplies whatever positive value the efficacy and effectiveness of the regime might achieve. It insures effectiveness even in the absence of desirable efficacy, and contributes to the ultimate outcome: persistence and relative stability of the regime. Should the value of legitimacy (the result of positive minus negative values among different sectors of the population or for key sectors) be close to zero, or negative, the failures of efficacy and effectiveness would be compounded. We might represent the relationship as follows:

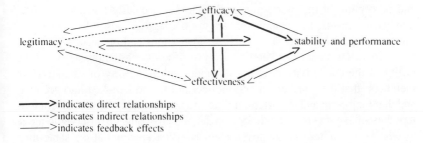

——————>indicates direct relationships
-------->indicates indirect relationships
——————>indicates feedback effects

The more positive the values on each of the relations, over time, the greater the stability and performance of the regime. What we do not know is how much each of those direct, indirect, and feedback relationships contributes. To express it graphically, we do not know how thick or thin the connecting arrows would be. Regimes that, to an outside observer, appear to be attaining the same levels of success or failure in handling problems, but that initially enjoyed different levels of legitimacy, do not seem to suffer the same consequences. Because of this, the circumstances surrounding the instauration of a regime and its initial consolidation become very important when and if it faces serious crises. Seen in this light, the particular historical origins of the Weimar Republic and its initial failures might account for its final breakdown in spite of its considerable success in the mid-1920s. Unfortunately, we have neither developed the systematic indicators nor collected the data over time on the legitimacy of regimes that would test hypotheses of this type.

Members of society, and today this implies a large collectivity, grant political power to the authority in a regime to pursue the satisfaction of their material and ideal interests. No one can deny that the ruling group is likely to pursue its own material and ideal interests, but they are unlikely to retain legitimacy if they pursue them exclusively or at too heavy a cost to broader segments of the society. Accountability, introduced by elections in democratic politics, makes it necessary for the leadership to demonstrate that they are pursuing collective goals acceptable to the majority without representing excessive deprivations for their opponents, even when they might represent a heavy burden to particular minorities. The response of society at large to the policies of its rulers is obviously not the same as that of an objective expert observer, and the success of a ruler might be based more on convincing society that the goals pursued are in its interest than in their actually being so. However, there is evidence that the people can be fooled some of the time but not all of the time.

While in theory the interests of the collectivity, or at least of a majority, constitute the yardstick for measuring the performance of the regime, the level of organization and consciousness of different sectors in the society varies considerably, as Mancur Olson has shown.[19] This makes the interests and perception of the more organized sectors particularly relevant. In addition, governments, like enterprises, are not necessarily judged by their short-run performance—particularly when the institutions and the leadership enjoy trust, i.e., legitimacy. The Paretian analysis of utility has emphasized that the utility of the collectivity does not coincide with the utility of its individual members, that there are direct and indirect utilities to be taken into account, and that long-term and short-term utilities do not coincide, etc. Considerations like these make it very difficult for even an objective outside observer to judge to what extent a democratic government is efficacious and at the same time responsive to an electorate. In addition, the problem is often compounded by the debate over whether it should be responsive to the electorate or should comply with the democratically taken decisions of the members of the governing party, in view of the pressures for internal party democracy. In addition to being responsive to the demands of a broad electorate and to the party membership, democratic governments cannot ignore the demands of key well-organized interests whose withdrawal of confidence can be more decisive than the support of the electorate. To give one example: policies that produce the distrust of the business community and lead it to an evasion of capital, even when those policies are supported by a majority of the electorate, might create a serious threat to a regime.

Given the interdependence, and in many cases, the dependence, of societies and states, the response of leading actors in the international political and economic system becomes another factor in judging the efficacy of policies. All this points to the complexity of a theoretical and empirical definition of the efficacy of a government or regime. Certainly, regimes and governments must serve collective goals, but as an already extensive literature on the functions of the state shows, those goals are far from being a fixed object of agreement.[20] They are historically conditioned and defined at each point in time by the political leadership and the society, particularly its organized forces. They represent constantly changing challenges. It is in clarification of these goals that the literature on the revolution of rising expectations (i.e., the increasing diffusion of institutions from one to another society or the internationally established standards of performance) becomes relevant. Social scientists impressed by the undeniable importance of economic and social policies in contemporary societies have, however, neglected consideration of some of the basic functions of any political system, past or present, particularly the problems of maintenance of civil order, personal security, adjudication and arbitration of conflicts, and a minimum of predictability in the making and implementation of decisions. Many of the regimes that failed because of a loss of efficacy did so because of difficulties at this level rather than because of their handling of more complex problems.

Efficacy, therefore, refers to the capacity of a regime to find solutions to the basic problems facing any political system (and those that become salient in any historical moment) that are perceived as more satisfactory than unsatisfactory by aware citizens. Many people, however, are likely to be neutral or indifferent toward many policies, and thus the total evaluation of the perceived efficacy of a regime is complicated by ignorance of the full significance of those responses for the stability of regimes. And further, contrary to the democratic dogma of one man/one vote, as Robert Dahl has already emphasized, the intensity of responses to policies cannot be ignored.[21] This becomes particularly important on considering the response of key, strategically located social groups or institutions, which in pure democratic theory should not be a consideration for the politician but in fact are central to his decision-making. Fortunately, the efficacy of a regime is judged not by the actions of a particular government over a short span of time, but as the sum of its actions over a longer period of time compared to the performance of different governments likely to be more satisfactory to one or another segment of the society.

Efficacy is judged over a long period of time.

This represents a special disadvantage for new regimes facing serious problems during the period of consolidation, since their governments cannot point to past achievements as proof of the regime's efficacy in the face of their presumably temporary failures. The problem becomes even more serious when the preceding regime has considerable efficacy to its credit, efficacy to which its remaining supporters can point.[22] Newness is a disadvantage that must be overcome, although the dynamics of regime change suggest that regime breakdown results from loss of legitimacy, and that the fall in and of itself enhances the legitimacy of the new regime. In the short run, however, the process of establishment may lead to a loss of efficacy or at least a discrepancy with the expectations created, and therefore a considerable drop in legitimacy before consolidation is achieved. If we were to draw the curves of these changes for different societies, we would find quite variable patterns within this general mode. In this regard, it is important to keep in mind, as Otto Kirchheimer has stressed, that a new regime's constituent acts in terms of policy are decisive for its consolidation.[23]

This leads to the importance of the formulation of the initial agenda of a new regime, the implications of its output for different sectors of society, and the consequent shifts in amount and intensity of legitimacy granted to it. That initial agenda is by and large in the hands of the leadership. The leadership can also delineate the conditions for solutions that will avoid both otherwise inevitable disappointments and the mobilization of intensive opposition, which in the consolidation phase will not be limited to the government but will extend to the regime. An adequate analysis of the means-ends relationships (the compatibility of the use of certain means with other ends and conflicts between possible ends) becomes crucial. This requires political intelligence, adequate information, and honesty in the perception of conflicts of ultimate values. In any case, outcomes beneficial to particular groups in society are likely to be delayed because of the difficulty of implementation at this stage. While efficacy is likely to be judged by outputs, sometimes the neutralization of potential opponents of the regime is of equal or more importance than the immediate satisfaction of those who have granted legitimacy to the new regime on the basis of their expectations.

Democratic regimes face more difficult problems in this respect than non-democratic regimes: the implications of their policies are visible to everyone, because of the freedom for criticism and information, which limits the regime's manipulation of the perceptions of society. It is in the area of "reform mongering," to use Hirschman's phrase, that democratic leadership must prove its ability.[24] If regime change were associated inevitably with a widespread revolution of rising expectations, the problems for a new regime might prove almost unsolvable. This result is generally modified by the "tunnel effect" (again a description by Hirschman), in which satisfaction of the expectations of some sectors of the society gives hope to others who do not see immediate outputs to satisfy their demands.[25] In sum, an intelligent formulation of the agenda, adroit management of the process of reform mongering, and immediate achievements in a particular sector that may serve as constituent acts for the new regime can make the problem of efficacy more manageable than seems possible at first.

We shall return to the issue of regime efficacy when we take up the solvability of problems confronting a regime and how they can become unsolvable, thereby contributing to the process of breakdown.

Legitimacy and efficacy, therefore, are analytically distinguishable dimensions that in reality are closely interrelated in ways about which we know very little. In what way does legitimacy facilitate efficacy, and to what extent, in different types of regimes and with different levels of legitimacy, does efficacy contribute to legitimacy? These are central questions in the study of the dynamics of regimes, but until recently they have received little comparative research.[26]

The effectiveness of regimes is still another dimension, though it is not often treated separately from efficacy, probably because it is a dimension at a lower level of generality and is therefore more difficult to distinguish empirically from legitimacy. "Effectiveness" is the capacity actually to implement the policies formulated, with the desired results. The fact that even the best laws are worthless if unenforceable falls within this concept. Despite widespread consensus about the goals to be pursued, and even about the means to be used, those goals, and above all, the means, can actually turn out to be unavailable, inefficient, and subject to delay and resistance in the process of implementation. At this point, perhaps more than at the point of policy formulation, discrepancies between expectations and satisfactions emerge, and dissatisfaction arises. Such ineffectiveness weakens the authority of the state and, as a result, weakens its legitimacy. Ineffectiveness also raises questions about policies that had been perceived as efficacious. Here again, new regimes face particular problems, since they have not yet assembled the administrative staff necessary to implement policies. During the initial phase, leaders are not in full command of the necessary information. The initial surge of support for the regime, plus the disorganization and weakness of the opposition, leads them to underestimate the resistance their policies are likely to encounter. Further, their self-righteousness as successors to a despised regime leads them to disregard even the valid arguments of the opposition, thereby increasing such resistance. As exemplified by the Socialist response to the agrarian reform failures of the leftist bourgeois-Socialist government in Spain in 1931–33, ineffectiveness is likely to split the regime-building coalition. Ineffectiveness is also likely to encourage illegitimate resistance to the decisions of the government. In this context, the maintenance of order in the implementation of decisions becomes central for the authority of regimes. Later we shall turn to a particular type of ineffectiveness, the inability to impose order or legal sanctions against those turning to private violence for political ends.[27] As all theorists have emphasized, the *ultima ratio* of legitimate authority is the use of force. A democratic leader—in fact, any leader—must be able to say: "My obligation under the Constitution and the statutes was and is to implement the orders of the legitimate authority with whatever means are necessary and with as little force and civil disorder as the circumstances permit and to be prepared to back them up with whatever other civil or military enforcement might have been required."[28]

All theorists of revolution, particularly the revolutionaries themselves, agree that the inefficient use of force, or reluctance to use it, is decisive in the transfer of legitimacy to the opponents of the regime.[29] At this point the decisive question posed by Pareto becomes relevant: "How can one incline people who would otherwise be neutral in the struggle to condemn resistance on the part of the governing powers and so to make the resistance less vigorous; or at a venture to persuade the rulers themselves in that sense, a thing for that matter that is not likely to have any great success in our day, save with those whose spinal columns have utterly rotted from the bane of humanitarianism."[30] Ineffectiveness of governments makes the question of legitimacy salient, particularly to those in charge of enforcing the law and defending the regime. This is an extremely complex problem in the process of breakdown of regimes and will be discussed at length later on.

The combination of these three dimensions produces an eight-fold typology of situations, the consequences of which should be analyzed in detail in the light of empirical situations. The realization that in any particular case we would need the aggregate patterns not only for the whole society but for particular segments of it, and, in some cases, the perception of these dimensions by key actors and political institutions, indicates how complex the analysis of the dynamics of regimes and their breakdowns can become.

Party Systems and the Instability of Democracy

Party systems in Western democracies are the result of long-term, complex historical developments, and therefore it is difficult to define the extent to which the same factors account for the emergence of different types of party systems and durable democracies.⟨Undoubtedly, the same structural factors that account for crisis-ridden democracies also account in large part for extreme, polarized, centrifugal multiparty systems. However, party systems are the result not only of structural factors but of institutional factors like electoral laws, the actions of political and social elites, the diffusion of ideologies, or *Zeitgeist* at the time of the instauration of democracy; they can also be considered as an independent or at least an intervening factor in the crisis of democracy. It is in this context, the character of party systems and party competition, that the consequences for democratic stability of electoral systems—in particular, proportional representation—have become the subject of scholarly debate.⟩

Two-party systems (to use an operational definition like that provided by Giovanni Sartori), could and can be found in only a small number of democracies.[31] Historically, the United States, the United Kingdom—with the exception of some periods of transition—and New Zealand, strictly defined, are the only extant two-party systems. (One might add Australia and Canada, which function as such.) In twentieth-century continental Europe, only pre-1923 Spain could be considered a two-party system at the parliamentary level (but not at the electoral level, particularly regionally). A number of smaller European democracies might have developed into two-party systems, had they retained single-member majority voting, but the introduction of proportional representation prevented such a development. Austria, which today functions as a two-party system, could not be considered as such in the period between wars, particularly around 1930.⟨In Latin America, Colombia and Uruguay could be considered two-party systems, even though the latter has features that should qualify that statement.⟩Outside the West, only the Philippines and Iran might at some time have qualified.

⟨ If we ask to what extent the pattern of political competition in two-party systems has contributed to democratic stability, our first impression is clearly positive, even though Spain in 1923 (with the reservations noted), Colombia in recent decades, and more recently, Uruguay and the Philippines, would suggest that such a party system does not prevent breakdown. It should be noted that in the case of these and other Latin American democracies, another factor might have to be taken into account: the presidential system.

⟨ It is perhaps no accident that when a two-party format is subject to maximal ideological distance and centrifugal competition, it is either destroyed or paves the way to a confrontation that takes the shape of civil war. This was the case in Colombia and perhaps in other Latin American countries. Republican

Spain, thanks to an electoral system that gave a heavy advantage to the largest pluralities and therefore to two major electoral coalitions, tended toward the two-party format, with the consequences, noted by Sartori, for highly ideological polities. In such a context, extreme multipartism, with all its costs, is the survival solution. It is no accident that fear of polarization inclined the Spanish Cortes to opt for proportional representation, rather than a single-member district system, in 1976, despite the fear of party fragmentation.

Continental European countries and Chile—the most stable Latin American democracy—were multiparty systems, albeit of very different sorts. A number of them have been, since the freeze in the party systems around World War I, moderate multiparty systems; that is, in Sartorian terms, they have fewer than five parties (which count to form coalitions or have blackmail potential). Specifically, they are Belgium and Ireland (three-party format); Sweden, Iceland, and Luxembourg (four-party format); Denmark (four-party until the 1950s, five afterward); and Switzerland, the Netherlands, and Norway (five-party format). (Norway and Sweden have had long periods of social democratic predominance, since 1935 and 1932, respectively.) All are systems with governing coalitions within the perspective of alternating coalitions, without sizable or relevant antisystem parties (except Belgium in the 1930s), with all their relevant parties available for cabinet coalitions or able to coalesce as oppositions, and with unilateral oppositions. They are characterized by 1) relatively small ideological distance among their relevant parties; 2) a bipolar coalitional configuration; and 3) centripetal competition.

This was not the case in the Portuguese Republic, Italy after World War I, Weimar Germany, France under the Third and Fourth Republics, the Republic in Spain, Finland, Czechoslovakia, the Baltic states, Eastern European and Balkan countries in the intermittent democratic periods, or Chile before the fall of Allende.

Certainly, comparison between countries with moderate nonpolarized multiparty systems and those having extreme multiparty systems suggests that moderate multiparty systems are associated with stability of democracy. Only in Belgium (at a moment when one could speak of a five-party system, with 11.5 percent of the vote going to the Fascist Rex and 7.1 to the Flemish nationalists) was democracy close to being endangered.

Of the thirteen relatively institutionalized democracies with extreme multiparty systems (leaving out Poland, Hungary, and the Balkan countries), seven were victims of a breakdown due to internal causes; one (Czechoslovakia) succumbed to a mixture of external and internal factors in 1938; two (Finland in 1930–32 and France in 1934) came close to a breakdown; and in 1958 the Fourth Republic escaped that fate through reequilibration. To these cases we could add Chile in 1973. There is, however, Italy, which since 1945 has been the archetypical case of multiparty system that has not experienced a breakdown, though it may be described as "surviving without government."

It seems clear that the two main types of multiparty systems distinguished by Sartori are not unrelated to the problem of democratic stability. Sartori rightly notes that segmented extreme multiparty systems whose parties locate themselves on more than one dimension, not competing between themselves since they have assured ethno-cultural, territorial, or religious electorates—Israel, Switzerland, and the Netherlands for example—constitute special cases. If they are not considered, the relationship between instability and extreme multipartism becomes even more salient. (It is impossible and unnecessary to present here his sophisticated analysis of the dynamics of extreme, centrifugal, polarized, ideological multiparty systems.)

Polarized pluralism is a system of five or more relevant parties (that is, with "coalition use" or "power of intimidation") characterized by the following:

1) The presence of antisystem parties (which undermine the legitimacy of the regime)

2) Bilateral oppositions (counteroppositions that are, in constructive terms, incompatible)

3) The central placement of one party (the DC in Italy) or of a group of parties (Weimar)

4) Polarization, or the positioning of the lateral poles literally two poles apart, due to ideological distance

5) The prevalence of centrifugal rather than centripetal drives in the electorate

6) Ideological patterning as a *forma mentis* rather than a pragmatic mentality differentiating parties

7) The presence of irresponsible oppositions, due to peripheral turnover rather than alternative coalitions, persistent opposition of antisystem parties, and semiresponsible opposition of those flanking parties forced to compete with them

8) The politics of outbidding.

It is the dynamic characteristics that account for the potential for breakdown in these systems: specifically, the polarization, the centrifugal drives, and the tendency toward irresponsibility and outbidding.

Another way to clarify the problem would be to study those extreme multiparty systems (in Sartori's sense) that resisted or have continued to resist their course toward breakdown for a prolonged time; specifically, the Third French Republic, the Fourth for many years, and Italy after 1945. Both Giuseppe Di Palma and Sartori himself have pointed out some of the factors involved.[32]

Undoubtedly, the experience of nondemocratic rule and the fear of it lead a large proportion of the voters to continue to give their support to the "Center" as a safe position, the one that best assures the survival of existing democracy, despite their disillusionment with its performance.

Is there a way out of the dynamics of extreme, polarized, multiparty systems? Sartori points—with skepticism—to a process of relegitimation of the antisystem parties. This process requires the antisystem parties to relegitimate, among their own followers, the system and the system parties. Such a process, he argues, would need to be visible, not based merely on invisible understandings (a point also made by Giuseppe Di Palma). Even if an antisystem party makes an effort in this direction, it is still not assured that it will be credible to both its opponents and its own followers, since it follows a long period of reciprocal delegitimation. A centripetal convergence at the invisible level of parliamentary cooperation, local politics, interest-group compromise, clientelism, and patronage can counteract the centrifugal systemic characteristics and insure "surviving without governing." Ultimately, however, it might not prevent a continuing process of deterioration, particularly in the context of violent antisystem activities of groups on both sides of the spectrum and in the face of "unsolvable problems." Let us retain for our analysis the idea that extreme multipartism alone does not determine the breakdown of democracy, but it does increase its probability. The case of Italy shows that such a system can last many years without resulting in that fatal outcome.

To approach the breakdown, the antisystem parties must act clearly as a disloyal opposition, and those flanking them must act as semiloyal parties when the Center (party or parties) loses strength when confronted with electoral defeat, faces "unsolvable" problems, or loses the will to govern. Sartori has analyzed *why*, in extreme multiparty systems, such situations are likely to develop (in part due to the dynamics of party competition), but it is our task to show more concretely *how* the process takes place.

Disloyal, Semiloyal, and Loyal Oppositions

Changes in regime occur with the transfer of legitimacy from one set of political institutions to another.[33] They are brought on by the action of one or more disloyal oppositions that question the existence of the regime and aim at changing it.[34] Such oppositions cannot be repressed or isolated; in a crisis they can mobilize intense, effective support; and by a variety of means they can take power or at least divide the allegiance of the population, which can lead to civil war. In certain unique circumstances, rulers selected by democratic means, faced with what they perceived as massive disloyal opposition, have been able to modify the democratic rules of the game and reequilibrate democracy by themselves, thus creating a new regime. Such a modification occurred during the transition from the Fourth to the Fifth Republic in France, and in Finland in the thirties. (For an analysis of the latter, see the chapter by Allapuro and Allardt in this volume.) It is not unlikely, as the case of Estonia shows, that they might try to save the regime from the immediate threat of a disloyal opposition by changing it in an authoritarian direction.

⟨No regime, least of all a democratic regime, which permits the articulation and organization of all political positions, is without a disloyal opposition. On the other hand, in most societies, the existing regime tends to have the benefit of the doubt, or at least the neutrality, of large sectors of the society. Except in crisis situations, this allows it to isolate and otherwise discourage disloyal oppositions, which are usually minorities and assume importance only in the process of breakdown.⟩ These facts give semiloyal oppositions a decisive role in the process of the loss of power by democratic regimes and implementation of a semi- or pseudo-legal takeover. Semiloyalty is particularly difficult to define, even *a posteriori*. The borderline between loyalty and ambivalent or conditional loyalty is not easy to draw, particularly since the democratic process strives to incorporate outsiders into the system as a participating loyal opposition⟨ In a political system characterized by limited consensus, deep cleavages, and suspicion between leading participants, semiloyalty is easily equated with disloyalty by some of the participants, while others dismiss or underrate such fears and emphasize the potential for loyalty of those suspected of ambivalence. This ambiguity contributes decisively to the crisis atmosphere in the political process. But to understand this concept fully, we must first define disloyal opposition.⟩

⟨ Certain parties, movements, and organizations explicitly reject political systems based on the existence of the authority of the state or any central authority with coercive powers. An example would be the pure anarcho-syndicalists, who certainly consider themselves disloyal to any democratic parliamentary regime and await the historical opportunity for their utopian revolution.⟩

Another obvious source of disloyal opposition would be secessionist or irredentist nationalist movements whose goal is the establishment of a separate new state or union with another neighboring nation-state.[35] However, it is not always easy to identify a secessionist party, since such groups generally start out by claiming to advocate cultural, administrative, or political autonomy within state or federal institutions. It is sometimes difficult to distinguish the rhetoric of nationalism compatible with a multinational state from appeals to create a separate nation-state, particularly when this rhetoric is propagated by parties that operate in both the regional and national political arena and employ a different style and a division of roles in their leadership. Such parties are often exposed to outbidding by extremists and activists, who seize upon the rhetoric of the broader movement and major parties to force them, in crisis situations, into actions that are, or appear to be, disloyal to the state rather than the regime. They are certainly likely to be perceived as disloyal even when they are only semiloyal. Principled commitment to a single overriding goal or the interest of a minority nation or a cultural and linguistic minority population leads such parties to be extremely opportunistic in relation to the regime-sustaining forces, which contributes to the distrust with which they are often perceived. The cooperation of such parties with the democratic regime, given their obvious ambivalence toward the state and the regime and their long-range commitment, grants those disloyal opponents of the regime who are strongly committed to the persistence of the state an opportunity to question the loyalty of the regime parties cooperating in these efforts to reach consociational solutions. In crisis situations, extremist ultraloyalists who are opposed to the regional nationalists' demands for autonomy find an opportunity to ask embarrassing questions, quoting nationalist rhetoric and demanding public declarations of loyalty to the state, which they conceived as a nation-state. Refusal becomes an argument against the regime parties cooperating with the nationalists. It also pushes the ambivalent nationalist into more disloyal, or apparently disloyal, positions.

Small extremist parties can be allowed a principled opposition, even a radical and violent one; but when such parties gain widespread support, infiltrate or control major interest groups, and begin to be perceived as serious contenders for power, they are likely to convey equivocal messages in order to maintain their radical opposition to the system while claiming to aim at a legal access to power. A plebiscitarian conception of democracy, identification with a latent majority, and disqualification of the majority as being illegitimate allow these parties to assert their ultimate claim to power, and the boundary between disloyalty and semiloyalty becomes confusing for many participants. In this sense, Fascist and particularly Communist parties after World War II were disloyal in a very different way from the anarchists, the antiliberal and antidemocratic monarchists in the nineteenth century, and some national liberation movements. This ambivalence of antisystem parties, which were at one point or another defined as disloyal, has made possible the legal takeover of power and destruction of democracy as well as the slow, complex process of integration into a competitive democratic system. The Fascist parties in interwar Europe and the Communists in the limited competitive democracies of Eastern Europe after World War II are prime examples of disloyal oppositions that protested against accusations of disloyalty while advocating destruction of the system as rightfully legal participants. And certain Socialist parties in the late nineteenth century and pre–World War I Europe were perceived at the time as disloyal oppositions because of their Marxist ideology, while they were in fact being slowly integrated into democratic politics.[36] Similarly, some of the political movements identified with the Catholic church and inspired by the fulminations against the liberal democratic state of the *Syllabus* were to become the strongest supporters of various democratic political systems in the second half of the twentieth century. What would be an effective "litmus test" of loyalty to a democratic regime? An obvious possibility is public commitment to legal means for gaining power, and rejection of the use of force. Ambiguities in such public commitment are certainly prima facie evidence of semiloyalty, but not always, as we shall see, of disloyalty.

Under certain circumstances, when the authority of the state is unable to impose the disarmament of all participants in the political process and to defend all parties against the violence of any other, it becomes easy to claim that paramilitary organizations and threats of force are purely defensive or preventive measures. In societies in which the armed forces traditionally act as the moderating power and intervene in the political process, parties may claim that some of their mobilizational measures are only defensive and supportive of the regime. Again, this blurs the distinction between disloyalty and semiloyalty, as various participants define the actions of the parties quite differently.

Another basic test might be rejection of any "knocking at the barracks" for armed forces support. Again, in an unstable situation in which a number of participants in the political process are perceived as disloyal, even loyal, regime-supporting parties would be tempted to establish such contacts with the army command or factions in the army close to them. In that case, the criterion is somewhat ambiguous, since even the system's supporting parties are likely to seek out support in the event of a crisis that might strain the expected normal loyalty of the army to the regime.

Another criterion would be denial of legitimacy as participants in the political process to parties that claim to be loyal participants, parties that have the right to rule thanks to the support they received from the electorate. One example of this would be the *retraimiento,* a traditional pattern of opposition behavior in Spanish and Latin American politics that involves a withdrawal from the legislature and a refusal to participate in parliamentary debates or in free elections, and results in delegitimation. The use of mass pressure by trade unions, taxpayers, or citizens in the form of strikes or mass protests disrupting the operation of government would be another indicator of disloyalty. But again, such actions are not unambiguous, since even system-supporting parties may turn to such tactics when they feel that there is no opportunity for fair and open competition in the elections. System parties, when faced with a formal, legal takeover of power by what they fear is an antisystem party, find such tactics the last recourse for defense of the system. How are we to judge such behavior without a judgment about the loyalty of those against whom those actions are directed?

Another closely related indicator would be the readiness to curtail the civil liberties of the leaders and supporters of parties attempting to exercise constitutionally guaranteed freedoms. To interpret that criterion rigidly would deprive democratic regimes of many legitimate defense measures. Certainly many of the measures, like the prohibition of uniforms, limitations on huge mass rallies in public places, strict control of the right to own weapons, and censorship of incitement to violence, can be construed as an illegitimate limitation of civil liberties and will make governments imposing them vulnerable to accusations of slowly eliminating democratic freedoms.

Obviously, blanket attacks on the political system rather than on particular parties or actors, systematic defamation of politicians in the system parties, constant obstruction of the parliamentary process, support for proposals made by other presumably disloyal parties with disruptive purposes, joint actions with other presumably disloyal parties for disruptive purposes, and joint actions with them in crisis situations and in toppling governments without any possibility of constituting a new majority are all typical actions of disloyal oppositions.[37] However, some of this behavior is occasionally characteristic of parties that we would not go so far as to label disloyal.

Strife between parties, efforts to discredit opponents, and the characterization of other parties as representatives of narrow interests in conflict with the public interest are normal, natural, and legitimate actions within the democratic process. Style, intensity, and fairness in conducting these actions mark the distinction between loyal and disloyal oppositions. Typically, disloyal oppositions picture their opponents collectively as instruments of outside secret and conspiratorial groups—communism, the Masons, international capitalism, the Vatican, or foreign powers.[38] Since corruption is likely to become particularly visible in democratic politics, oppositions have an opportunity to discredit as corrupt not only the leaders (and their associates) but the whole party, and in the case of a disloyal opposition, the whole system. When system parties turn to that style of politics, it is prima facie evidence of the shift toward semiloyalty. A significant correlation exists between the image of politicians or the political class as a whole as dishonest and the readiness to turn to violent means, as table 1, showing responses to survey questions by those supporting non-Communist parties under the Fourth Republic, shows.[39]

Table 1. Survey Questions: Are Politicians Honest? Should Your Party Seize Power by Force?

	Should Take Power by Force	Should not Take Power by Force	No Answer	(N)
Majority of honest men	3.6%	74.8%	21.6	329
Minority of honest men	7.1	58.8	34.1	364
No honest men at all	16.1	22.3	61.6	112

NOTE: Those asked these questions were supporters of parties other than the Communists in France.

Public scandals involving system party leaders, if intelligently exploited by a disloyal opposition, provide an opportunity to establish bridges between other system parties and the disloyal opposition on the legitimate claim of exposing the corruption of the system. They contribute in this way to the drift into semiloyalty.

We have listed a number of criteria for disloyalty, none of which appears as necessary and sufficient, since opposition groups that might ultimately be integrated into the system as loyal supporters occasionally engage in them, particularly when faced with political forces they perceive as disloyal. Certainly, disloyalty in parties that do not publicly commit themselves to the overthrow or total transformation of the system if elected is not unambiguous. It is this basic ambiguity of the definition of disloyalty, except in the case of small, highly ideological and principled antisystem antidemocratic parties, that makes it so difficult to defend an embattled democracy and to prevent the silent takeover by antidemocratic parties. The combination of a number of such indicators would allow us to describe the syndrome that defines political forces disloyal to democracy. Even if it is not disloyal, a political force with such characteristics can reasonably be perceived by some of the participants as disloyal to competitive democracy and by many more as semiloyal.[40] When a party that has engaged in one or several of the patterns described is in power, its opponents will seize upon those actions to label it a threat to democracy, even when it has refrained from taking power undemocratically or suspending the democratic electoral process and the necessary civil liberties. In such a situation, who is to decide whether that label is an alibi for the antidemocratic ambitions of the opponents or the basis for an *ademocratic* defense of democracy? The outcome of the conflict would seem an obvious test, but unfortunately, a defense of democracy by ademocratic means is not likely to bring about its reequilibration.

The intermittent presence, in attenuated or ambivalent form, of some of the characteristics we have used to define political forces disloyal to a democratic system, is characteristic of semiloyal parties and actors as well. In addition, certain other characteristics define semiloyalty, foremost of which is the willingness of political leaders to engage in secret negotiations to search for the basis of cooperation in government with parties they themselves (and others acting with them) perceive as disloyal. This indicator does not imply the intent to overthrow the system or change it radically, since it might be motivated by the desire to integrate into the system forces that can be coopted, moderated, or sometimes split through such negotiations. There is evidence that more often than not such efforts contribute to the demise of democratic institutions. But there are also cases in which they have helped to neutralize and ultimately defeat antidemocratic forces, sometimes, as in Finland, at the cost of some deviation from pure liberal democracy.[41]

An indicator of semiloyal behavior, and a source of perceptions leading to questions about the loyalty of a party to the system, is a willingness to encourage, tolerate, cover up, treat leniently, excuse, or justify the actions of other participants that go beyond the limits of peaceful, legitimate patterns of politics in a democracy. Parties become suspect when, on the basis of ideological affinity, agreement on some ultimate goals, or particular policies, they make a distinction between means and ends. They reject the means as undignified and extreme, but excuse them and do not denounce them publicly because of agreement with the goals so pursued. Such agreement in principle and disagreement on tactics is a frequent indicator of semiloyalty. Political violence, assassination, conspiracies, failed military coups and unsuccessful revolutionary attempts provide the test situations for semiloyalty. Unequal application of justice to the illegal acts of different disloyal oppositions contributes decisively to the image of semiloyalty. The granting and refusal of amnesty to opponents of a democratic system provides another test situation. Governments that face disloyal opposition at either end of the spectrum, or have gained support from parties who acted disloyally against a previous government, are in a difficult position when forced simultaneously to assert their authority and expand the basis of support for their rule. In such circumstances, the suspicion of semiloyalty becomes almost unavoidable. Parties of heterogeneous composition, recruited by the fusion of different elements, inheriting leaders and supporters from a previous regime, and divided by factional conflicts, find themselves divided and in ambiguous positions when faced with such situations. Because the lack of discipline in parties makes it difficult for the leaders to disavow the statements and actions of their lieutenants and subleaders, their own public statements might not be sufficient to gain confidence. A frequent pattern (one seen during the interwar years in Europe) is the radicalization of the youth and student organizations of parties that the mature party leadership cannot disown without losing some of its most active and enthusiastic followers. The same sometimes holds for special-interest groups closely tied with political parties.

Ultimately, semiloyalty can be identified by a basically system-oriented party's greater affinity for extremists on its side of the political spectrum than for system parties closer to the opposite side. Unfortunately, in a highly polarized society, when extremist parties engage in violence and have the power to attract segments of the system parties or their electorate, system parties are likely to behave in such a way that they seem semiloyal even if they are not. One characteristic of the final stage of the breakdown process is that to one degree or another the parties whose main aim should be to defend the authenticity of the constitutional, democratic, political process engage in actions that justify other participants' perception of them as semiloyal.

The crisis situation, provoked by unsolvable problems and by the presence of a disloyal opposition, with its voluntarism and sense of historical mission, promising *hinc et nunc* a solution to all those problems without feeling obliged to spell out specific policies that could gain majority support, creates the conditions for the emergence of semiloyal political forces. The antecedents of that development, however, can often be found in earlier, more stable periods. One that often characterizes newly established democratic regimes is the tendency of its supporters to identify democracy with their own particular social and cultural policies. The majority, in setting up a new democratic regime, is impressed by its own strength and by the weakness of the social strata identified with the preceding regime. It often feels that its task is not only to establish an institutional framework for democratic processes but to anchor in the constitution many very specific policy decisions. On that basis, any opposition to those policies is perceived as antidemocratic action rather than as an effort to change the decisions of the temporary majority. Such an exclusionary definition of democracy pushes what could have been a loyal opposition into semiloyalty as we have defined it. The Spanish Republicans' expression "A Republic for the Republicans," meaning by "Republicans" those who supported unconditionally the policies enacted by the founders of the regime, certainly had that effect. Many democratic reform parties tend to misperceive any opposition to a particular constitution or to basic social, economic, and religious changes as antidemocratic, when there would be room for such opposition in a democratic constitutional framework.[42] Democracy, particularly in its difficult early years, requires mechanisms that allow the opposition, if willing to abide by the law, to have a significant share of power. The inclusion of the opposition could be accomplished by offering them an opportunity to participate in the legislative process through committee work, by granting the interest groups linked with them access to those in power, and sometimes allowing them representation in corporative institutions. Decentralization, or local and regional self-government, can reduce the feeling of those not participating in the foundation of the new regime that they have been excluded. The systematic exclusion or discrimination against the partisans of the opposition in many realms of public life, such as the bureaucracy, the armed forces, or the administration of interventionist economic policies, might push those ready to become a loyal opposition into semi- and disloyal positions. Such elements might easily become the active supporters of semiloyal positions that could contribute years later to the breakdown of the regime.

Much sophistication is needed in the initial stage to discern which groups and individuals from the opposition, especially the latter, can become loyal or honestly neutral but compliant citizens. The temptation of *ressentiment* politics is often too strong to allow such a process of integration. Undoubtedly, unnecessary personality conflicts within the political elite tend to hamper the future cooperation of government and loyal opposition. Those conflicts are not so great when the democratic political system has evolved slowly out of a more restricted political system like a semiconstitutional monarchy with representative institutions, an oligarchic democracy in which democratic reformers had already participated in a minority role, or a system of dual authority like that of India before independence. They are exacerbated when the instauration of democracy follows a prolonged period of authoritarian rule that provided no opportunity for the emergence of counterelites, and the interaction in certain political arenas such as legislatures, municipal governments, or interest-group bargaining.

Instauration of democracy after an authoritarian regime allows its founders to question the credentials of many interests in the society, among them opposition leaders who collaborated with the fallen regime. In this respect, regimes succeeding highly ideological and exclusionary totalitarian regimes that possessed a well-defined political elite of the activists of a single party face a less difficult situation than those succeeding amorphous authoritarian regimes. If the founders of a new regime label any person who has been connected with the previous regime unfit to participate in the democratic process unless he denies his past, they contribute to a self-fulfilling prophecy of creating a semiloyal or even a disloyal opposition. In a democracy, loyalty to a new regime cannot be applied retroactively, except in extreme cases when the general consensus of the society rejects the previous regime almost unanimously on moral grounds. In this respect, the posttotalitarian democracies in Germany and Italy after World War II found themselves in a situation quite different from that of the post–Primo de Rivera Republic in Spain or the post-Perón democracy in Argentina. In both latter cases the authoritarian regime had been welcomed by a large part of the population; and despite the errors that led to its breakdown, its legitimacy, rejected according to widely shared liberal democratic standards, was not rejected on moral grounds by large segments of the population. The understandable exclusion of the regime's former supporters did not allow them to become a semiloyal opposition with a chance of integration, much less part of the loyal opposition.

Spain's return to democracy in 1976–77, after the death of Franco and almost forty years of authoritarian rule, presents special characteristics. Like Turkey's return to democracy in 1945, the change is unique in that it has taken place not through a breakdown of the regime but through the intiative of the rulers, under internal and external pressure. To date (after the 1977 election), it has led not to a transfer of power to the main opposition forces but to a power-sharing process legitimated by a free competitive election. The change through *reforma* rather than *ruptura* poses special problems for new democratic institutions. These institutions were born according to the formal constitutional amendment procedures of the Franco constitution, yet they countervened the spirit of the fundamental laws in a process that has much in common with the antidemocratic perversion of democratic constitutions, but with the opposite result. Some of the problems for the cases of instauration and restoration noted above in the Spanish case acquire new and unexpected complexity.

One of the central characteristics of a crisis democracy is that even the parties that have created the system tend to deviate from the ideals of a loyal system party when they encounter hostility among extremists on either side of the spectrum. The constraints of the situation push everyone toward some form of semiloyalty, even semiloyalty to the democratic system.

Certainly the actors in the political process of a crisis-ridden democracy are even less able than the historians or social scientists who follow them to agree on which other participants are loyal, semiloyal, or disloyal. This ambiguity ultimately makes the defense of the democratic political process very difficult and contributes a great deal to the slow but apparently inevitable process of breakdown. The presence of one, but particularly two, polarized disloyal oppositions with significant support tends to lead to the emergence of semiloyal political actors, to their polarization, and to the increased isolation of those unequivocally loyal to a democratic competitive political system.

It is this inherent ambiguity of the political process in crisis situations that so often makes simple moral judgment after the fact so dangerous and sometimes unjust. At the time, only intensive interaction and communication within the elites interested in the survival of the system on a basis of mutual trust can create a consensus on loyalty and disloyalty. Only under those conditions can the willingness to put loyalty to the system before other commitments, ideological affinities, and interests be achieved.

What emerges at this point is a definition of political forces constituting the loyal opposition to a democratic regime. Ideally, such forces would be characterized by:

1) An unambiguous public commitment to achievement of power only by electoral means and a readiness to surrender it unconditionally to other participants with the same commitment.

2) A clear and uncompromising rejection of the use of violent means to achieve or maintain power except by constitutionally legitimate means when faced with an illegal attempt to take power.

3) A rejection of any nonconstitutional appeal to the armed forces to gain power or to retain it against a loyal democratic opposition.

4) An unambiguous rejection of the rhetoric of violence to mobilize supporters in order to achieve power, to retain it beyond the constitutional mandate, or to destroy opponents, including even ademocratic or antidemocratic opponents. The defense of democracy must be carried out within a legal framework, more or less narrowly construed, without arousing popular passions and political vigilantism.

5) A commitment to participate in the political process, elections, and parliamentary activity without setting up conditions beyond the guarantee of the necessary civil liberties for reasonably fair democratic political processes. Requiring an agreement on substantive rather than procedural policies is in principle incompatible with the assumptions that the minority must respect *pro tempore* the decisions of the majority and that the majority in turn must respect the right of the minority to reverse its policies, except in the realm of requirements for competitive politics, should it become the majority.

6) A willingness in principle to assume the responsibility to govern or be part of the majority when no alternative government by system parties is possible. An even more stringent but not unreasonable requirement would be the willingness to participate in government when it might otherwise be weakened in face of crisis.

7) The willingness to join with opponents ideologically distant but committed to the survival of the democratic political order. (This requirement is more stringent and perhaps unreasonable.) It might apply even against parties that are closer ideologically but are committed to helping to undermine the democratic political process by the use or the rhetoric of violence and an effort to curtail the civil liberties of a legitimate opposition.

8) A rejection of secret contacts with the disloyal opposition and a rejection of its support when offered in exchange for tolerance of its antidemocratic activities. In principle, an effort to make the boundary between the system party, broadly defined, and antisystem parties as clear as possible both publicly and privately is a major characteristic of system-loyal parties or political forces.

9) The readiness to denounce to a legitimate democratic government the activities of opposition forces or the armed forces aiming at the overthrow of that government. This criterion is certainly stringent, and is more difficult to apply, since it goes beyond the unwillingness to participate in such conspiratorial activities to requiring support for political opponents facing a threat.

10) A commitment in principle to reduce the political role of neutral powers, like presidents and kings, the judiciary, and the armed forces, to narrow limits to assure the authenticity of the democratic political process.

If those ten requirements had to be unambiguously satisfied, the number of loyal participants in the democratic political process in most societies undergoing a serious crisis would be greatly reduced. In fact, in some of the cases we shall analyze, like that of Spain in the 1930s, the reader of the detailed historical record might come to the conclusion that there were *no* major parties and key leaders that would fully satisfy that ideal definition. In any democracy in crisis we will discover taints of semiloyalty even in the parties most committed to democratic stability, parties which under normal circumstances would satisfy our criteria.

It might clarify the distinctions we have made to link them with Richard Rose's analysis of the authority of regimes.[43] System parties and the loyal opposition contribute, through high support and high compliance, to the full legitimacy of the regime authority. The open and sincere disloyal opposition is characterized by low support and low compliance. Their aim is the repudiation of the regime, but failing in this, their actions make it semicoercive. When the opposition is strong and is faced with a strong regime, its actions tend to make the regime coercive. Modern disloyal oppositions, however, in the ambiguities of their appeal, give the impression of mixed support, and they vary their degree of compliance in accordance with the strength of the regime parties, the cohesion of government forces, the opportunities presented by the situation, and the unsolvable problems. Their presence results in partially legitimate, divided, or disrupted regimes, terms coined by Richard

Rose that convey a sequence in the loss of control faced by the system parties confronted with the refusal of the disloyal opposition to comply, as regime authority becomes less efficacious and effective. It is, however, the semiloyal opposition, with its relatively high, or at least mixed, compliance, rather than the disloyal opposition, that pushes regimes into the partially legitimate and divided authority situation. The regimes we shall study in this volume found themselves in these intermediary situations, moving from partial to divided legitimacy, sustained as coercive or semicoercive, and finally becoming disrupted and repudiated or isolated as in the Rose typology. It is our contention that the conditions leading to semiloyalty, or even suspicion of semiloyalty, by leading participants in the political game, opposition and government parties alike, account for the breakdown process almost as much as the role of the disloyal oppositions.

[handwritten margin note: Conditions leading to semiloyalty or disloyalty are held as responsible for breakdown as the presence of the opposition groups]

Crisis, Loss of Power, Breakdown, and Takeover

We have attempted to underline the probabilistic and changing character of legitimacy, efficacy, and effectiveness of a political system at any moment in its development. We have also characterized the loyal and disloyal oppositions to a regime, particularly a democractic regime, as well as the type of opposition that we call semiloyal, which will play a decisive role in our description of the process of breakdown. We have not yet mentioned the sequences of events, the dynamic processes that serve to explain why these dimensions display different characteristics at different times in a democratic political system.

The kinds of events that contribute decisively to destabilization, overthrow, and in some cases reequilibration of a democracy have in recent years been the object of considerable theoretical discussion and empirical research concerned particularly with the onset and characteristics of violence and resultant governmental reactions. Cabinet stability as both an indicator and a cause of the crisis of regimes has been studied empirically, but not in connection with the broader problem of the stability of regimes.[44] Other aspects, like the implication for democratic stability of different party systems and the links between party systems and electoral systems, have, since the important work by Hermens, been the object of much debate.[45] Unfortunately, there has been relatively little research on the links between economic and political crises, despite the importance assigned in the Marxist theoretical tradition to the economic crisis under capitalism, the resultant breakdown of democracies, and rise of fascism to power.[46] There is no lack of theoretical or empirical research on these and other processes contributing to the breakdown of democratic regimes. However, the insights derived from such analyses have not been integrated into a more complex descriptive model. That, in our view, can only be derived from an inductive analysis of at least some of the paradigmatic cases that historical research has so thoroughly documented for us. In this respect, the work of Bracher has broken new ground.[47] The fascination with political violence, expressed most notably by American social scientists in response to recent events in the United States, and the concentration of intellectual efforts on the study of the unstable polities of the Third World have led to an unfortunate neglect of other aspects of the process of crisis, breakdown, and reequilibration. Let us not forget that while civil strife and political violence have caused the overthrow of government and regimes in many countries, the relatively stabilized democracies, which are the object of our study, have fallen in a more complex process in which the violence was but one contributing factor. Perhaps violence triggered those other processes, but only in cases of direct military intervention has the use of organized violence sealed the fate of regimes. Even in those cases, as more sophisticated recent analyses of the role of the military in politics have shown (see Alfred Stepan's study of the Brazilian military), military action was the result of the complex process of decay of the existing regime.[48]

The one-sided focus on the actions of the opponents of the regime, particularly radical and violent movements, the frustrated segments of the population, and military intervention, has tended to overlook the actions of those interested in the survival of the democratic regime, and the many organized social forces and institutions that might have been favorable or at least neutral toward the regime but finally withdrew their support from it. Social scientific analysis seems to alternate between an emphasis on the ultimate structural strains (particularly social-economic conflicts, inequality and rapid social economic change, and dependency) and on the period of open strife that immediately precedes the breakdown. This dual emphasis neglects the political process itself, functioning under constraints and often contributing to the conditions that generate rebellion and violent conflict. We agree with Charles Tilly when he writes:

Despite the many recent attempts to psychologize the study of revolution by introducing ideas of anxiety, alienation, rising expectations, and the like, and to sociologize it by employing notions of disequilibrium, role conflict, structural strain, and so on, the factors which hold up under close scrutiny are, on the whole, political ones. The structure of power, alternative conceptions of justice, the organization of coercion, the conduct of war, the formation of coalitions, the legitimacy of the state—these traditional concerns of political thought provide the main guides to the explanation of revolution. Population growth, industrialization, urbanization, and other large-scale structural changes do, to be sure, affect the probabilities of revolution. But they do so indirectly, by shaping the potential contenders for power, transforming the techniques of governmental control, and shifting the resources available to contenders and governments.[49]

Our main focus, therefore, will be on the incumbents and their actions, their formulation of the agenda for the regime, their way of defining problems and their capacity to solve them, the ability of the pro-regime forces to maintain sufficient cohesion to govern, the willingness of the democratic leaders to assume the responsibilities of power, the rejection of the temptation to turn to ademocratic political mechanisms to avoid making political decisions, the readiness to turn to nonpartisan sources of legitimacy, the willingness to coopt or enter coalitions with the disloyal opposition rather than turn to the defense of the regime, the narrowing of the political arena after the loss of power and the onset of a power vacuum, as well as such inadequate responses to the crisis atmosphere as badly timed elections and inadequate use of the coercive resources of the state. It is such political processes that give rise to, strengthen, and embolden the disloyal opposition and contribute to the emergence and wavering actions of the semiloyal opposition. It is also in such political processes, initiated by the incumbents, that we must search for an explanation of the processes of reequilibration or transformation of democratic regimes that allow them to overcome serious crises. They also contribute much to explaining the results of the breakdown process and the reasons the succeeding regime takes one or another configuration.

The Instauration and Consolidation of Democratic Regime and Its Future Stability

The history of the democracies whose fate concerns us here highlights the importance of the inauguration and initial consolidation of the regime for its future capacity to confront a serious crisis. It is no accident that constitutional debates use so much energy in building new democracies and that politicians and traditional political science devote so much attention to the virtues and defects of the subsequent constitutions. In retrospect it is easy to blame certain constitutional provisions, such as the famous Article 48 of the Weimar constitution, for consequences that were not intended and probably could not have been foreseen when the provision was being drafted. The same could be said of the electoral law of the Spanish Republic, hastily enacted without much discussion by the provisional government, or the absence of a real executive in the Estonian constitution.

The drafting of a constitution, however, is not the only process in democratic regime-building that has long-term implications. Equally important, or more so, and not just for the provisional or first government but for the regime itself, is the initial agenda adopted at that stage. For that agenda often creates expectations that cannot be satisfied within the existing framework and soon become the source of semiloyalty on the part of forces involved in the regime-building process. In fact, the initial agenda can contribute to consolidation of basic positions toward the legitimacy of the regime, particularly when that agenda is defined not as a government program but as a substantive part of the constitution that is difficult to reverse by simple majorities. Furthermore, when a regime changes, a large proportion of the population is expectant or neutral, rather than strongly committed to those who have established it or loyal to the regime that has fallen. This is particularly true when the party system of the new regime was not able to crystallize under its predecessor, as is the case when a preceding authoritarian regime did not allow organized opposition to participate in any way in the political process. In such an event, attitudes toward the legitimacy and efficacy of the new regime are quite likely to be permanently shaped by its initial steps. At this stage the new rulers can enact policies that have a socially constituent character, creating a solid basis of support among those benefiting from them. It is also a moment when they can minimize the concerns of those neutral to the change of regime but worried about its implications.

The leaders of a new democratic regime are likely to be tempted to place all unsolved problems of the society on their agenda simultaneously, presumably to maximize support, without realizing that in doing so they also maximize the number of persons likely to be affected negatively by their reforms. The simultaneous placement on the agenda of many complex problems whose solution has been protracted for decades is likely to overtax the resources of a leadership with little administrative experience, limited information, and scarce financial resources. Even assuming that the solutions proposed were all efficacious, the regime might be equally damaged by lack of effectiveness in implementing them quickly. In the process it would have raised unduly the expectations of its supporters and aroused the fears of those who expected to be negatively affected by the reforms without reaping the support of those intended as beneficiaries.

Why should this be the recurrent pattern in new democratic regimes? In our view, there are multiple causes. One is the tendency to blame the accumulation of problems on neglect by a previous regime rather than on the intractability of social reality. The initial euphoria and the image of widespread support, measured more by the crowds on the street and the festive mood than by votes, often give rise to the feeling that with good will all problems can be solved, particularly after a long dictatorial period. The leaders of the democratic regime have usually had time to think about the problems of the society and their solutions, but have not confronted the task of formulating them in precise terms and linking the solutions with specific facts in the face of the resistance they are bound to encounter. New democracies generally are instituted by coalitions in which even minor groups whose strength is still unknown might be represented and want a hearing. In multinational societies, the crisis of the previous regime and the unsettled future tend to weaken the central government and activate autonomist or even secessionist demands that have to be put on the agenda. The new leaders also might feel somewhat uncertain about their future strength, should the social forces identified with the previous regime recover their organizational capabilities, and therefore wish to legislate and even add their programmatic aspirations to the new constitution.

This desire to achieve fundamental changes in a society by legislative fiat is not matched by the resources to implement such changes. Any change of regime is likely to have some disturbing effects on the economy, and not infrequently this leads to a withdrawal of public credit, evasion of capital, and reduction of investment. Combined with the limitations in the attention span of government leaders absorbed in constitutional and legislative debates, who are coping with an unfamiliar bureaucratic machinery assisted by an unqualified staff, implementation of such a broad agenda tends to become practically impossible. The resulting disappointments and frustrations are likely to lead to conflict within the initial regime-building coalition.

Many of the changes that new regimes introduce are of a symbolic character: the change of flags, for example, is generally deeply felt only by a minority, but is hurtful to those attached to tradition.[50] Such changes may arouse enthusiasm at first, but since they do not represent tangible advantages for the supporters of the new regime, they do not constitute the kind of breakthrough or policies that might attach large sectors of society to the new order. They do become, however, an important rallying point for the disloyal opposition and contribute to a semiloyal attitude on the part of political groups hoping to win supporters from the disloyal opposition.

The new rulers also have a tendency, probably based on their feeling of moral superiority, to waste energy in what might be called *ressentiment* politics against persons and institutions identified with the old order.[51] This would consist in petty attacks on their dignity and their sentiments. Such measures are likely to be echoed at lower level, in administration and local government, particularly in the rural societies, and may even be used in settling personal accounts.[52]

Bitterness over symbolic changes and the emotional costs of *ressentiment* politics are not easily forgotten.[53] In such policies lodge the roots of disloyal opposition and latent ambivalence toward the regime that may become manifest years later at the time of serious crisis. Often the psychological shock that accompanies a regime change is greater than the actual social changes, and this accounts for the intensity of the hostility on the one side and the disillusion with the actual changes on the other.

In the consolidation phase of the democratic regime, therefore, an intelligent analysis of the political costs and benefits of each policy is particularly important. What is at stake is not the success or failure of a particular government but the formation of basic predispositions toward the regime. Much can be gained by selecting a limited number of problems and instituting at a relatively rapid pace reforms that will benefit and reassure a significant number of people at the cost of disappointing small and sometimes highly visible minorities. This is not easy, but some regimes have been fortunate. For example, in some Eastern European countries large-scale agrarian reform was possible because the large landowners were members of a foreign ethnic minority.

Foreign policy issues very often represent a heavy load for a new regime, which might at first find itself in relations of dependency with other countries. This was a particularly acute problem for Germany, Austria, and other successor states after World War I. The formation of the German Republic and full democratization accompanied defeat and the acceptance of the Versailles treaty, which led many Germans to deny legitimacy to the new regime and to feel a nostalgic loyalty to the old order.[54] This was particularly true among army officers and civil servants, and even among Protestant clergymen and professors. The statehood imposed on Austria, and the Allied prohibition of any unification with Germany, restated whenever the Republic found itself in economic difficulties, contributed to the illegitimacy of democracy among those with strong pan-German sentiments. As Paolo Farneti shows in his analysis of the Italian crisis, the cleavages created in all camps by interventionism, the cost of the war, and disappointment with the fruits of victory contributed much to the inability of Italian democracy-in-the-making to face the difficult readjustments in its economy and social structure after the war.[55] Dependency and economic nationalism in Latin America after World War II played a similar role.

Such issues seem to be particularly intractable in the consolidation phase because the identity of the state is at stake. Foreign commitments cannot be as easily reversed as internal policies, since they depend on outside powers not under the control of any future government, and a disloyal opposition can easily blame the system rather than a particular government for the constraints. In addition, the process of international negotiation is likely to lead to contradictory and ambiguous positions. Statements made for home consumption may differ from those made at the conference table, compromises are accepted with mental reservations, and expectations of revision begin to develop. An extreme example of such ambivalence can be found in the Fiume policies of Italian governments and the German rearmament in contravention of the Versailles treaty, policies that contributed to the emergence of highly politicized paramilitary groups that were tolerated by the authorities despite their protestations to the contrary.

Incorporation of Those outside the Regime-Founding Coalition

In our view, a new democratic regime can count on the intense loyalty of those who opposed the previous regime and first assumed power to create the new institutions. Contrary to what many analysts in sympathy with them believe, the number of those continuing to accord legitimacy to a fallen regime generally tends to be small. After all, the fall of the previous system is usually the result of a shift in loyalty by citizens of weak commitment, by the apolitical, as a result of a crisis of legitimacy, efficacy, or effectiveness. If these citizens had not shifted their allegiance, the previous rulers would have been able to resist the change and to rally at least enough support for a violent conflict with the challengers; this in turn would probably have led to a period of dictatorship rather than to a democracy. The period of consolidation, therefore, is largely a struggle for the allegiance of those relatively uncommitted sectors of the population.

Unorganized, disoriented, even fearful at first, the uncommitted might join, or at least vote for, the more moderate sectors of the new regime-building coalition (in Germany, this was expressed as support for the Deutsche Demokratische Partei). But given the opportunities for political organization provided by democracy, the growing awareness of their distinct interests, and the almost inevitable failure of governments in this phase, these unattached sectors may regroup behind new parties or even political figures from the previous regime. These new political forces are likely to question the decisions made in the name of a temporary majority and to win considerable support in subsequent elections. The problem for the builders of a new democracy is whether these challengers should be admitted as fully legitimate participants in the political process, or if their participation should be conditional upon their full acceptance of the changes introduced by the regime founders. This issue can divide the founding coalition and the political elite. Setting a high threshold for participation beyond the electoral level and excluding the principled opposition from many arenas is likely to make future cooperation in a crisis situation difficult. In some cases potentially loyal democrats, who do not support the substantive content that others want to assign to the regime, are pushed into a principled opposition and cooperation with the disloyal opposition, a tendency sometimes reinforced by the electoral system. An image of semiloyalty might result, and those parties at the other end of the spectrum in the regime-founding coalition will veto the entry of such forces into the government and violently criticize more centrist parties who are ready to incorporate them into the system. The result is a strong centrifugal tendency on the part of all participants and the fragmentation of parties (in extreme cases this becomes the "impossible game" as described by O'Donnell in Argentina after Perón).[56] The immediate result is deep personal antagonism between parties and the impossibility of forming a broad, shifting center coalition against extremists on both sides of the spectrum. Ultimately, the result is a weakening of the legitimacy of democratic institutions and the growth of both disloyal and semiloyal oppositions; if a serious crisis were to require a regrouping of the democratic forces, it might prove impossible.

We must emphasize the importance of defining the disloyal opposition clearly and at some stages isolating it politically, but this process can be successful only if there is concomitant readiness to incorporate into the system those who are perceived as at least semiloyal by some sectors of the regime-building coalition. Statesmanship, flexibility, and timing are badly needed at this stage, because the process of incorporation, which does not always represent a gain in efficacy, can be very important in the process of legitimation of an open, competitive democratic system.

Here again, continuity between the democracy and its predecessor regime is important. Political elites that have become known to each other, even developed a certain trust over years of parliamentary life, are more likely to accept such an incorporation than are adversaries who have no shared experiences in politics. The contrast between the relative stability gained by the Weimar Republic and Austrian democracy in the mid-twenties, and postwar Italy and Spain in the thirties, can be explained in part by the relative continuity of parliamentary personnel.[57] The emergence of two new parties, the Populari and the CEDA in the Latin democracies, representing a new form of Catholic participation in political life under a young, unknown leadership, was upsetting to the bourgeois liberals, while the effect of the Zentrum in Germany and the Christian Social Party in Austria was just the opposite.

Legitimation as a Problem for Democratic Leadership

In our introduction we advanced the proposition that, the higher the commitment in numbers and intensity to the legitimacy of the regime, the greater its capacity to survive serious crises of efficacy and effectiveness when confronted with unsolvable problems. Faced with problems of equal dimensions, a regime with a high commitment to its legitimacy has a higher probability of survival than a regime without such commitment. Legitimation, therefore, becomes the primary task of democratic leadership. Establishing the initial agenda in the period of consolidation, the negative consequences of *ressentiment* politics or foreign policy liabilities, and the difficulties of incorporating potentially loyal forces not in the regime-building coalition are all clearly relevant to this problem. There are, however, other dimensions that should be analyzed in the study of the consolidation of new democracies in order to account for their later weakness.

Democracies build their legitimacy on the basis of loyalty to the state or the nation. In fact, certain sectors of society, particularly army officers, civil servants, and sometimes intellectual leaders, feel a stronger identification with the state or the nation than with a particular regime and reject in principle the partisan identification of the state. Unless the regime is the result of widespread social mobilization of a revolutionary type that allows it to reject the idea of continuity of the state, this represents a serious problem.

One solution that can be successful is a purge of those unwilling to make a clear and public commitment to the new political order. In fact, many analyses of the breakdown of democratic regimes blame the founders for not having carried out democratization (or penetration in terms of democratic loyalty) of such institutional sectors. However, to do so in modern societies that recognize acquired rights, and in liberal democracies that guarantee freedom of opinion, is far from easy. It is likely to result in ambivalent and contradictory policies that, instead of achieving the desired result, arouse the indignation of those affected.

In this area symbolic discontinuities that force public expression of otherwise unarticulated beliefs about the legitimacy of the system become crucial. Minor issues, like the changes of flag, national anthem, or ritual invocations, can often create incidents and bitter feelings, and help to crystallize a disloyal opposition. Supporters of the new regime sometimes find satisfaction in those symbolic changes, but in our view, stabilization requires the maximum continuity in the symbols of the state and the nation as a consensual basis between those committed to the new regime and those they intend to incorporate into it. Such symbolic continuity will make regime acceptance easier by avoiding emotion-laden choices in the initial stages.

Another serious problem faced by regimes, particularly democracies, in building legitimacy is posed by failure to define the boundaries of the state and the nation. In situations like that in Northern Ireland, any form of democratic majority rule will be perceived by the minority as oppression, and the loyalty of part of that minority to another nation-state makes even consociational solutions difficult. The question is not one of the legitimacy or instability of a democracy, but of a state. The problem exists, though in less extreme forms, for many multinational states, particularly when the state or the regime has been built largely by one nationality, like the Serbs in pre–World War II Yugoslavia, the Czechs in Czechoslovakia, and, historically, Castile in Spain. In these cases, full democracy must allow the expression of the nationalism of the periphery, and it permits not only autonomist or federalist demands, but secessionist demands. Tolerance for these demands, which is sometimes imposed by the international situation, creates almost unsolvable problems for democratic leadership.

The same is true when the nation is conceived as a broader entity than the state, including people across the borders. Such a conception accounts for the ambivalent loyalty of nationalistic pan-movements to democratic institutions, because these movements question the regime leadership's acceptance of the existing state boundaries. As the experiences in Italy, Austria, Weimar Germany, and to some extent Finland, show, the democratic leadership, with its ambivalence imposed by international pressure as well as its own policy commitments, contributes to the delegitimation of the system or at least some of its participants. Perhaps the democratic leadership in these situations ought to emphasize the state as a source of legitimacy, rather than the nation.

Let us not forget that Fascist appeal is based on the need to affirm national solidarity against a system that allowed cleavage and conflict of interest within the society. That democratic forces could, generally through gross distortion, be relabeled as anational because of their international links was important in the process of delegitimation of many democracies. This would apply to socialism with its heritage of internationalism and pacifism; the Catholic parties' links with the Vatican and an international church; the bourgeois business parties and their links with international capitalism; and obviously international communism, which, without sharing in power, was a beneficiary of democratic freedom.

All studies of revolutions and of the intelligentsia have pointed out the latter's role as legitimizers and delegitimizers of authority. As Pareto noted, ideological formulations by the clergy, and by intellectuals in the modern world, have been extremely influential in convincing the subject classes of their right to rebel and the ruling classes of their moral right to use force to defend an existing order.[58] Given the role of universities in the training of government officials, judges, and lawyers, and the role of journalists and writers in shaping public opinion in societies that guarantee freedom of thought and expression, the distribution of attitudes toward the legitimacy of the regime and the various sources of attack on it is bound to depend to a large extent on the climate created by these different sectors of the intelligentsia and the academic community. It could be argued that each political and social movement has the support of its own intellectuals, who therefore play only a secondary role, but Karl Mannheim, with his idea of the free-floating intelligentsia, would argue the contrary.[59] In spite of the partisan attachments of its intellectuals, every society includes some intellectuals whose standing, on account of their creativity or their literary, aesthetic, or scientific achievements, is special, and whose critiques of the political order play an important role in any legitimacy crisis. Freedom of expression, the rejection of censorship, the right to cultural, religious, and political heterodoxy, and the freedom of dissent have been and continue to be central concerns for intellectuals and artists. No political system today gives greater scope to those freedoms than democracies, even without discounting the occasional deviations from those norms, and certainly the regimes whose breakdown concerns us here allowed intellectuals to pursue their creative role. It should follow that a liberal democratic system would find widespread support in the intellectual community, but the evidence on the political role of intellectuals in many democracies in crisis shows that few took upon themselves the public defense of democratic liberal institutions against opponents from either the Right or the Left.

There are obviously important national differences resulting from the cultural, religious, and institutional traditions as well as differences between the academic, the literary, and the artistic sectors, and there are also differences that reflect changing historical situations. However, many of those differences account more for the Left/Right orientation of the intellectual critique of liberal democratic politics, their sympathies for one or another type of extremism, than for their identification with regime-supporting parties. The paradox of the ambivalence of intellectuals toward liberal democracy is not easy to explain,[60] although the following factors might account for it: the elitism of intellectuals and their hostility to the average man, who is, after all, the average voter; their dislike for politics based on self-interest rather than on ideas of a better society; their dislike for the professional politician, whom they often consider their inferior and whose lack of understanding and respect for their ideas they resent; and their unwillingness to accept the bureaucratic discipline and *cursus honorum* of modern mass parties, which reduces their influence as compared to that of trade union officials, men with experience in local government, or leaders of interest groups. Additional factors might be the frustration of intellectuals with the unwillingness of mass electorates and their representatives to devote resources to either high or avant-garde culture; their hostility to the influence exercised by powerful interests through the use of money for advantages in and through mass parties, in contrast to their own influence as men with creative ideas; the frustration of the expert with the pragmatic distortion of his best proposals; and last but not least, the bitter hostility against other intellectuals ready to serve those in power and subverting the critical role of the intelligentsia.

Even when intellectuals support the creation of democratic regimes, they soon adopt critical positions and withdraw from the political process. The literati, particularly artists, tend to become indignant with the banality of the routine political process. The second rank leaders of parties, the petty party officials, and the low-level rhetoric and demagoguery of electoral campaigns become the object of their ridicule. The *alltag* character of democratic politics contrasts with the potential for great historical transformations realized in other societies that serve as utopian points of reference. All such responses find an echo among students, and certain sectors of the educated and half-educated will simplify them to mobilize support against the system, which they feel has betrayed or failed to realize higher spiritual values, be they conservative or revolutionary. Those predispositions created by an intellectual climate are likely to reemerge for other reasons when the leaders of the regime fail in their tasks.

The ambivalence of many intellectuals toward competitive pluralistic liberal democracy has perhaps an even more profound origin. It is the basic moral ambiguity of a political system that legitimizes decisions on the basis of formal, procedural, legal correctness without distinction of content except respect for civil liberties and the equality before the law of all citizens, with no reference to substantive justice and no link to a system of ultimate values. In societies suffering from serious injustices and deep cultural cleavages, it is difficult to accord intellectual justification to a system in which the will of the electorate, the technicalities of the law-making process, and the decision of the courts can serve to maintain a social order that arouses moral indignation or, conversely, can allow a reformist majority to question an inherited value system. Democracy can be justified only by a particular turn of mind, founded, as Kelsen has already noted, on a certain relativism or on a pragmatism grounded in an empirical processing-coding based on an open cognitive structure, flexible elements, and weak affect, to use Sartori's expression.[61] It is far from evident that such an outlook will prevail when a society confronts difficult problems that cannot wait.

3.
The Process
of Breakdown

Unsolvable Problems and Crisis

Any political system, once established with a certain amount of legitimacy, can count on the passive obedience of most citizens and the more or less effective repression of violent challenges from a disloyal opposition by the forces of order. As long as the electoral strength or even the parliamentary representation of the disloyal oppositions does not constitute an absolute majority, and if the loyal parties agree on the desirability of the system's continuity, a democratic regime can survive. But before that point is reached, one or a number of crises will probably have undermined the consensus of the democratic parties and their capacity to cooperate. Such crises are the result of a lack of efficacy or effectiveness of successive governments when confronted with serious problems that require immediate decisions. In the last analysis, breakdown is a result of processes initiated by the government's incapacity to solve problems for which disloyal oppositions offer themselves as a solution. That incapacity occurs when the parties supporting the regime cannot compromise on an issue and one or the other of them attempts a solution with the support of forces that the opposition within the system perceives as disloyal. This instigates polarization within the society that creates distrust among those who in other circumstances would have supported the regime.

It is only a slight exaggeration to label such problems unsolvable, for a solution acceptable to a majority among the regime-supporting parties cannot be found, and meanwhile a large part of the politically and socially mobilized population becomes less willing to wait for effective action. This means that increasing numbers of the population withdraw legitimacy from the system and support disloyal oppositions, or at least advocate collaboration with them in search of a solution. In this context it is irrelevant that the problem might have reached such intensity because of the activities, particularly the violent activities, of the disloyal oppositions. In fact, the antidemocratic oppositions' strongest argument is their claim to be able to solve the problem and to obstruct any solution they find unsatisfactory. This process leads from the unsolvable problem to the loss of power, the power vacuum, and ultimately to the transfer of power or the polarization of society and civil war. There can be

50

no doubt that a polarized, centrifugal, multiparty system is both a consequence and a cause of such a process.

Given the constraints of the system, how does it happen that regimes come
to face problems that are unsolvable—or are at least perceived as such by a
majority? There are many reasons, and it would be presumptuous to attempt to
analyze them here in detail. Some are structural problems that perhaps no
regime can solve. Others might exceed the capacity of a regime trying not to
compromise democratic freedoms and processes. Still others might simply
become unsolvable because of the way in which the democratic leadership has
formulated them and its ability to implement certain solutions or overcome
certain constraints that should not be insuperable.[1] In societies, particularly
European societies, in which democratic regimes gained considerable stability, relatively few problems were of the structural type; many of the difficulties arose following decisions by the democratic leadership that made solutions
within the democratic framework impossible. Oversimplifying somewhat, we
can say that a regime's unsolvable problems are often the work of its elites.

Obviously some problems are caused by an absolute imbalance between a
society's needs and its resources that perhaps no government could resolve
without outside support. This is certainly the case in the poor, overpopulated
countries of the Third World, and no government committed to full respect for
democratic freedoms would be able to tackle them. These problems may
worsen if the structural difficulties are not recognized, if problems are blamed
on others, and if false hopes are created by the leadership. Intractable structural problems inherited from the past, however, might prove intractable only
in the short run, especially if the desired solutions are measured with reference
to other, more developed societies rather than with respect to the starting
point. Hirschman has rightly noted how a structural view of progress tends
toward a pessimism that discounts any relative progress and rejects anything
but an integrated, comprehensive, and simultaneous solution of all basic
problems.[2] Another fallacy would be the belief that no specific problem can or
should be tackled until power relations in the society have been completely
restructured and the groups perceived as obstacles to solutions have been
dispossessed or destroyed, without even exploring the possibility of solutions
bypassing or affecting those groups without destroying them. Ultimately this
is the position of maximalist marxist Socialism, convinced of the impossibility of cooperation with other parties within a democratic framework, unwilling to enter into the government and formulate specific solutions to pressing
problems, and even less willing merely to safeguard democratic institutions as
instruments of future solutions.

In an increasingly economically interdependent world, the solution of certain problems is beyond the decision-making capacity of many national governments. This has led and will increasingly lead to ultranationalistic and
voluntarist responses, which are likely to be associated with authoritarian
politics. There have been, and there will probably continue to be, conflicts

between states that might not be susceptible to immediate revision by peaceful means, or at least without the kind of mobilization of resources that would make a military threat credible. Democratic political processes make that kind of solution difficult and therefore expose a government committed to a revision of its international position and the boundaries of the state to principled attack by a nationalistic disloyal opposition.

A realistic appraisal of the situation and an unambiguous commitment to peaceful revision of the status quo, rather than the creation of ambiguous expectations through other solutions, might prevent many difficulties. Undoubtedly, as Clausewitz has emphasized in his classic analysis of war as the continuation of politics with other means, success depends on defining goals for the military leadership for which the political leadership can provide the necessary means, as defined by the military. If those means cannot be provided, pursuit of those goals must be renounced.[3] In fact, unless there is overwhelming consensus on the goals to be pursued by military means and success is relatively rapid, a democracy will face considerable questioning of methods like conscription, high casualties, and expenditures used to pursue a certain goal as well as increasing doubts about the value of the goal. In such a situation, democratic leaders may be tempted not to abandon the goal but to pursue it without demanding the necessary means from the society in the hope of reducing the opposition caused by the demands. This unwillingness to recognize the internal logic of the military instrument, to admit the impossibility of achieving military goals with the available means, is likely to have serious consequences for the stability of the regime. It means the inevitable alienation of the military leadership from the political leadership, because the military feels it has been made responsible for the failures of the politicians, who are unwilling to confront the society with the real choices.

Some of the most serious crises of democratic regimes have been caused by this kind of problem, particularly since democratic regimes must tolerate pacifists and even treasonous opposition to war. It was certainly a major contributing factor in the breakdown of the constitutional monarchy in Spain in 1923, in the final crisis of the Third Republic, which was provoked by the unwillingness of the army command to continue the war under a government moving outside metropolitan France, and in the rebellion that fortunately only led to the transformation of the Fourth into the Fifth Republic in 1958. This type of problem is not unique to democratic political systems, as recent events in Portugal show, but is particularly salient for them. It should be noted that the military challenge to civil authority is not necessarily based on a commitment to continue the war, but might in fact favor abandoning it in view of the impossibility of victory with the available means.

This example derived from the Clausewitz analysis exemplifies the basic source of unsolvable problems in our sense of the term—the setting by the political leadership of goals for which it is unable to provide the necessary means, and its unwillingness to renounce those goals once it becomes apparent that the means cannot be provided. That incapacity is often caused by the incompatibility of certain means with other goals that the leaders are either unable or unwilling to relinquish. In some cases, the leaders might be unaware of the impossibility of simultaneously pursuing incompatible objectives or values. Max Weber, in his *Science as a Vocation,* suggested that a central task for social scientists was to contribute to the rationality in human life by making explicit such conflicts between values and improving knowledge of the means-ends relations as well as of the indirect and often unanticipated consequences of using certain means.[4] The blindness of political leadership to some of these relationships springs from many causes, including ignorance and incapacity, although ideological rigidity, dependence on subleaders, expectations created in the electorate, and the constraints imposed by interest groups are the main causes. They can force the democratic leadership to face the difficult choice of pursuing ends and values to which it is committed, or to give them up, in part or temporarily, for the sake of the survival of democratic institutions.[5] Who is to argue that political leaders should sacrifice staunchly held policy goals, the interests of their followers, or their image of a good society for the sake of the persistence of political institutions that do not seem to serve the pursuit of those aims?

In view of this discussion, it should be no surprise that political leaders with strong commitment to an ideology or those identified with specific social interests are least able to give foremost consideration to the persistence of institutions. When ideological and social motivations become fused, as in the case of many Marxist Socialist leaders deeply concerned with the interests of the working class and the trade unions, or Catholic politicians combining an ideological view of society with an unquestioned loyalty to the church, unwavering commitment to a political system per se becomes extremely unlikely. The impossibility of solving a pressing problem within such confines leads easily to withdrawal from responsibility and semiloyalty to the system.

In a democracy, the leaders depend, particularly in a crisis, on the support of party organizations rather than the electorate. This often means responsiveness to the middle-level cadres (likely to be the most highly ideological) and leaders of special-interest groups, which makes the problem particularly difficult.[6] In some cases the increasing infiltration of interest groups at the grass-roots level by emerging leaders identified with one of the disloyal oppositions tends to further limit the political leadership's freedom of action in terms of system interests.[7]

Complex problems, particularly when faced by a fragmented leadership, lead to inaction or ambivalent solutions and afford the disloyal opposition the opportunity to attack the system and demand the power to implement simple solutions. Hitler stated it quite well when he said: "I will disclose to you what has raised me to my position. Our problems seemed complicated. The German people did not know what to do about them. In these circumstances the people preferred to leave them to the professional politicians. I on the other hand have simplified the problems and reduced them to the simplest formula. The masses recognized this and followed me."[8]

The capacity of governments to handle problems is obviously limited; it depends on alternative strategies in contriving reforms, as described by Hirschman, and most governments can handle only particular types of problems successfully.[9] In fact, it could be argued that shifting coalitions, and consequently unstable governments, in a crisis-ridden society might build up a better record for the regime than would the same political forces facing all the problems. However, government instability, irrespective of some of the positive consequences it might have in terms of efficacy, is perceived by the society as both a sign and cause of regime crisis.[10] Success in handling difficult problems sequentially with changing coalitions within the regime is largely a question of timing.

Unsolved structural problems, therefore, undermine the efficacy and, in the long run, the legitimacy of the regime, but they are rarely the immediate cause of the breakdown. It is only when they become acute and demand an immediate response that they can become unsolvable. This can be brought on by rapid and massive changes in economic conditions, such as a deep depression, rampant inflation, or a negative turn in the balance of payments, defeat or stalemate in war, or when dissatisfaction is expressed in more than anomic violence, generally under the leadership of a disloyal opposition and accompanied by mass mobilization. The most serious crises are those in which the maintenance of public order becomes impossible within a democratic framework: when the regime needs to be reassured of the loyalty of the forces of repression, when the use of such forces against one or another group becomes impossible without endangering the regime-sustaining coalitions, and when the disloyal opposition is perceived as capable of mobilizing large parts of the population, or strategically located sectors of it, unless the problem is solved.

In the last analysis the breakdown is precipitated by what the constitutional tradition calls "states of emergency"—the need for extraordinary powers, the state of exception. As Carl Schmitt noted, with considerable exaggeration but also with insight, the sovereign is the one who can decide in the state of emergency.[11] At this point, when the problems are beyond the democratic sovereign, the transfer of loyalties to another sovereign takes place. And in Tilly's view, this transfer, broadly speaking, defines revolution.[12] Either a regime change or a change within the regime that implies a decisive reequilibration must take place.

The capacity of the regime-sustaining forces to handle such situations, however, derives from the accumulation of the resources of legitimacy over time and the record of its efficacy in previous crises.

Albert Hirschman's theory of loyalty unexpectedly parallels the Weberian concept of legitimacy and our application of it to the problem of stability.[13] Hirschman notes how demand of a product—in this case, support for a regime—is always likely to be a function not only of current but also, to some extent, of previous quality, because of inertia and lags in perception. In our terms, legitimacy is a function not only of current performance but of previous performance. As he writes, "Loyalty strongly reinforces this influence of past performance of the firm or organization on present behavior of the customers or members." Where Hirschman says "loyalty," "organization," and "members" we would say "legitimacy," "regime," and "citizens." The central theme of his analysis is that as the result of loyalty, members will stay on longer than they would otherwise do, in the hope, or rather the reasoned expectation, that improvement or reform can be achieved "from within." In our context, they will not shift their support to the disloyal opposition, but will continue to support the regime-sustaining parties and hope for a recovery of efficacy or effectiveness. This gives them a chance to implement adequate policies or, if nothing else, to gain time, allowing circumstances beyond the control of the government to improve. In this instance, regimes with a long history of stability have an advantage over new regimes.

Different regimes might be equally unable to find adequate solutions to such problems as unemployment caused by depression. But the initial strength of the disloyal opposition's blaming the problem not on a particular government, but on the system, the difference in degree of mobilization and violence expected, and the extent of trust in the unconditional loyalty of the forces of order against any challenger can make the problem unsolvable in one case and just a crisis in another. In sum, it is not the technical characteristics of the problems but the political context in which they are placed, the constraining conditions on the regime, and the alternatives offered by the existence of one or more disloyal oppositions that ultimately trigger the process of breakdown.

Crisis Strata and Their Location in Society and Politics

The extent to which individuals can be mobilized for either mass movement or violent action against the regime in a crisis varies widely from one society to another. The recent literature on why men rebel has assembled considerable empirical evidence, using the theory of mass society and research on the psychological processes underlying aggressive responses as a starting point. Sociological analysis and descriptive studies have focused on the facilitating conditions, particularly those legitimizing violent action and those enabling the organization and the success of such action. Unfortunately for our purposes, the research has been either on historical cases like the French Revolution and its nineteenth century counterparts or on agrarian unrest in Third World countries.

There are no systematic comparative data on the role of crisis strata and their impact in the democracies included in our analysis.[14] We have some basic statistics on unemployment that permit cross-national comparisons, but no similar data on the social impact of the Great Depression on the independent middle classes or the peasantry and even less systematic data linking those economic and social changes with the rates of political mobilization, particularly in the form of paramilitary partisan organizations. While it is possible to use biographical data to trace the impact of World War I, civil strife in the postwar years, and nationalist mobilization to defend the borders and to fight the Ruhr occupation in creating the core of activists of the Nazi movement, particularly those engaging in violent actions, we have no comparable analysis for the origin of North Italian squadrismo.

The presence in the crisis-stricken social groups of individuals who have leadership qualities, free time, experience with discipline, and skills in the use of violence is particularly important in accounting for the nature of the disloyal opposition and its possible course of action. In this context, a crisis affecting the Spanish upper and middle classes including important sectors of the landowning peasantry under the Republic did not produce a political movement like Nazism or even Italian Fascism. In Spain, the lack of participation in World War I and the resulting absence of a veterans' generation and reserve officers of middle-class backgrounds, as well as the smaller number of students who had not completed their educations and were under- or unemployed, limited the size of the potential leadership cadres for a Fascist movement. Consequently, social classes affected by the crisis of the Republic and threatened by the mobilization of the working class could not rely on a large number of Fascist activists and therefore had to turn to the army to defend their interests.

Political Violence and Its Impact

Except for the intervention of the armed forces, the takeover of power from democratic leaderships has rarely been the result of a direct attack like that described in the manual on coup d'état by Curzio Malaparte.[15] Hitler did not move into the Reichskanzelei as the result of a putsch. And Mussolini did not march into Rome to storm the Quirinal at the head of the Fascist legions, but, summoned by the king, traveled in a sleeping car. Violence did, however, play a major role in the breakdown of these democracies, not so much in the actual takeover as in the process of limiting their efficacy, contributing to their loss of legitimacy, and creating a loss of power and power vacuum. Unfortunately, the rich body of research on patterns and causes of violence fails to link such patterns with their consequences for regime stability.[16] In fact, countries that typologies classify as unstable because of the amount of political violence that characterizes them have not suffered regime change, while others characterized by less violence have gone through deep crisis and even change. What is more, not infrequently the violence erupts only as a result of an attempted regime change.

The literature makes even less effort to analyze to what extent the growing violence or fear of it is the result of the actions of the authorities, except for exploring the now-popular thesis that the repressive actions of government tend to make more victims than do the actions of the challengers, and that this might contribute to the mobilization for further violence. Perhaps because the literature has concentrated on cases in which violence for political purposes or with political consequences was the expression of grievances that scholars have been ready to consider justified, attention has centered on the dysfunction of attempts to repress it. Little attention has been paid to situations in which the authorities, the police, and the judiciary, even though disapproving of violent political acts, dealt leniently with them because they felt sympathetic to the motives of those engaging in them or hostile to their victims.[17] Nor has the literature focused much on the impact of decisions concerning violence and its punishment on the political process and the relationships between parties and actors in the political system. In our view, some of the delegitimizing consequences of violence can be found in the area of decisions made in response to violence.

We refer to such complex decisions as whether an act is considered to be political or to represent social grievances, or as one conceived by irresponsible madmen or common criminals, irrespective of their claims and the perception of particular sectors of society; judgment about whether to stop the first outbreaks of violence or to allow its perpetrators recognition by negotiating with them; and decisions about the amount and type of force to be used to repress violence, in particular the use of police, armed forces, and paramilitary groups supporting the government. Further complex decisions involve the degree and type of recognition to be given to the representatives of forces of order who died in the performance of their duty; responses in terms of declaring various levels of emergency and restrictions of civil liberties; actions to be taken against leaders who may have allied themselves with those engaged in violence, particularly if they hold parliamentary immunity; and decisions about whether recourse should be to the ordinary or special jurisdictions in particular military courts when the events took place under states of emergency granting powers to the military. Decisions must be made as to readiness to pursue individual actors whose guilt can be easily established and who sometimes are responsible for real atrocities, but inability or unwillingness to pursue political leaders who supported the guilty parties but whose guilt cannot be proven; as to pardon or execution of sentences in such situations and resolutions of internal conflicts within the government coalition and between government and head of state in such matters; actions and legislation limiting the freedom of parties to engage in activities that are likely to produce situations of violence, like certain types of demonstrations, provocative marches, or the wearing of uniforms, and the right of civil servants, particularly members of the police and armed forces, to belong to certain parties; and ultimately, as to whether to outlaw certain organizations and even political parties because of their illegal acts and their threat to civil peace.

All these decisions can undermine or strengthen the legitimacy, efficacy, and effectiveness of a government in relation to different sectors of the society and the political spectrum. But the capacity to make such decisions with positive results depends largely on the previous legitimacy, efficacy, and effectiveness of both the government and the regime. This constant interaction in a changing situation makes it equally difficult for social scientists to advance general propositions and for the politicians to face such ambiguous situations.

What is most important is that when the violation of the laws and violence is intended for political purposes, is condoned by a leadership with considerable following, and is not condemned by large sectors of society (even when not approved by them), a regime, particularly a centralized government, must respond; and it cannot, as in private crimes or even anomic social violence, ignore the political implications of its decision. For in a society with disloyal opposition at either end of the spectrum, the regime-supporting forces can be sure that whatever decision they take will be exploited by one side or the other, or even both, to undermine regime legitimacy. In these situations the semiloyalty of some political groups or leaders is likely to manifest itself and contribute further to an atmosphere of distrust and polarization.

The individual chapters in this volume will give considerable evidence of how decisions in this area, in one way or another, have contributed to the loss of authority of democratic regimes and their ultimate breakdown, not always to the benefit of those who created those crises.

Loss of the Monopoly on Organized Political Force

A chief characteristic of the modern state is the monopoly of legitimate force in the hands of the police and the military under the direction of the political authorities. When the decision to use force cannot be made by the political authorities alone, but requires the consultation or agreement of those in control of that armed force, then the government is faced with a serious loss of legitimacy. The same holds true when a government allows organized groups with paramilitary discipline whose purpose is to use force for political ends to emerge in the society. Such groups are likely to become more and more autonomous, to develop their own ideology and purposes, and in general to be unresponsive to democratically elected governments. Not even paramilitary organizations, created with government approval by parties identified as supporters of the democratic regime in order to oppose a disloyal opposition and support the government in an emergency, seem to be either effective or desirable in a democratic political system. Certainly the tolerance of a democratic regime for the creation of paramilitary organizations by disloyal oppositions creates a most serious threat to its existence. This tolerance constituted a decisive factor in the disintegration of democratic rule in Italy, Germany, Austria, and to some extent, Spain.[18]

Unique historical circumstances contributed to the emergence of paramilitary groups in the Europe of the interwar years.[19] For example, in Germany, Austria, Finland, and the Baltic countries the defense of border areas, particularly those of mixed ethnic composition, was taken over by citizen guards, created more or less spontaneously under the leadership of volunteer, demobilized reserve or retired officers. The fact that some of those countries were new nations without a professional army accounts for this pattern. In northeastern Europe the borders were to be defended against the Soviet Union, a fact of importance in understanding the political orientation of the groups so formed and the veterans' organizations that maintained their traditions. In the case of Austria and Germany the defeat and disintegration of the army, the limits imposed by the victors on the army, and its role and size were other factors.[20] Those groups were directed not only against border threats but also against more or less successful revolutionary or pseudorevolutionary attempts, like the short-lived Kurt Eisner reign in Bavaria.[21] They were organized as a result of the fears aroused by the Russian and Hungarian revolutions.

Given their weak resources, these new democratic states had to tolerate and, in a number of cases, rely on the support of such irregular organizations. These groups, however, developed a spirit of their own and became the core of ultranationalist and rightist paramilitary groups that led the hostility against not only the Communists but also the regime-founding moderate Socialists. Their members were to become National Socialists, active in the paramilitary SA and SS. In addition, in later years the high command of the army, with some support from the government, decided that these organizations and the militant veterans' organizations could form both the core of a reserve army for internal and external emergencies and an instrument to circumvent the limitations on military training imposed by the Versailles treaty.

The same was true in Italy, where many army commanders and some governments closed their eyes to or even encouraged nationalistic paramilitary organizations, like those involved in D'Annunzio's Fiume expedition or the Fascists in the disputed Italo-Yugoslav border area, bypassing involvement of the armed forces in order to avoid the wrath of allies who opposed Italian demands. That ambivalence toward politically organized violence was later extended to the Fascists in their struggle against domination by leftist organizations in the countryside in the red belt of the Po Valley.

In all these cases, government tolerance of the violent acts of the disloyal opposition increased as a result of the ambivalence of the authorities, the potential cost of suppressing the opposition, the links between the opposition and the regular army due to the presence of many former officers among their leadership, and the fear of the organization of paramilitary groups by the Left in response to their actions. Furthermore, if the regime-supporting parties were to create their own paramilitary organizations, the decision to outlaw such organizations fully would have had to be applied to them too, and this was another policy that encountered resistance. In addition, in Germany the differences in the political composition of the governments of the German states and their policies toward such organizations impeded the development of a single unified policy. One of the most serious consequences of the government's loss of the monopoly over the armed forces was its resultant dependence on the army in matters of internal order. The army high command was thus included in decision-making concerning armed disloyal oppositions.

Another case in point occurs when democratic governments or party leaders question the loyalty of the state's armed forces or even of lower government units. They then attempt to combat that threat by creating, encouraging, tolerating, or even talking about the creation of nongovernmental armed forces like the workers' guards, the *grupos de onze* in Brazil, or the *cordones industriales* in Chile. It would seem that in a democratic framework, the capacity of political groups and nonrevolutionary governments to create such forces is limited. Before they can be organized, the military establishment, realizing the threat, will strike against such governments, probably with greater unity than would otherwise be the case. The same is probably true for any policy encouraging the politicization of soldiers or noncommissioned officers as a preventive policy against a military putsch. Such measures are a clear indication of the government's or the regime's loss of legitimacy among the armed forces and are only likely to accelerate and reinforce that loss. In a modern society with a well-organized, professional military, defeat and repression of such forces is the most likely outcome, if not civil war, should the police or sectors of the army remain loyal to the government.

Little of the analysis of violence in recent literature has considered this twilight zone of encouraged or tolerated paramilitary organizations that become political factors, probably because the amount of violence as measured by the usual indicators might be small. Even though systematic data are lacking, the standard indicators of civil violence for the last years of the Weimar Republic probably would be lower than for the early years, but the visibility of political armies and the inability of the government to reestablish its monopoly over organized force boded ill for democracy.

In this context it should also be emphasized that the political significance of violence by both challengers and government agents depends very much on the response to violence by the institutions that must sanction it: parliament, respected organs of public opinion, and spokesmen of the elite. One-sidedness in excusing or condemning such acts is both an indicator and a cause of loss of legitimacy of participants in the political process. Our chapter on the Spanish case illustrates how such a process creates unsolvable problems for a regime, and how intelligent participants realized that this would accelerate the process of breakdown unless drastic decisions were made by the regime's supporters to stop it.

Paradoxically, a democratic regime might need a larger number of internal security forces than a stabilized dictatorship, since it cannot count on the pervasive effect of fear. Its reactions to violence require massive but moderate responses; only numerical superiority can prevent the deadly reactions of overpowered agents of authority. It needs to protect not only government leaders but opposition leaders and even one group of extremists against another. Reequilibration of democratic regimes probably requires intelligent responses to such challenges, including in some cases a redefinition of the tolerable limits of civil liberties.

Democratic Crisis and Multinational States

One assumption of any working democratic political system is that the loyalty of the citizens to the state, irrespective of regime or government in power, should be greater than their loyalty to another state either existing or in the making.[22] The legitimacy of the state within its territorial boundaries is a prior condition to the legitimacy of any regime and is particularly important in the case of a democracy that must guarantee civil liberties to all citizens. In a multinational state, when across the border lies another state and that considers them irredenta with which a significant number of its citizens identify, stability is seriously threatened. In such a case, especially should a strong nationalist movement with more or less veiled secessionist aims exist, democracy and perhaps even the state may lose viability. A stable political system assumes that citizens in all parts of the country should feel bound by the decision of the authorities and not give their loyalty to another state.[23]

The basic assumption of the democratic political process is that today's minority might in the future either become a majority by convincing those in the present majority to agree with them, or hope to become a majority as a result of slow changes in the social structure. That was the case of the labor parties whose hopes were pinned on the growing class consciousness of the workers and/or the growing number of proletarians in the Marxist sense of the word, i.e., those without ownership of the means of production. The same would be true for ideological parties of one or another character. The situation is quite different in the case of ethnic, cultural, or linguistic minorities, unless they can hope to assimilate the majority or unless decisions on the policies affecting them are delegated to self-governing local bodies, where they would constitute the majority. Unfortunately, even that might not be a solution in societies in which the national minority that is a majority at the local level faces a large-scale minority in its own region without any hope of assimilating it. Consociational mechanisms can reduce the inevitable tensions in this case, but as any reader of the growing literature on consociational democracies will realize, the preconditions established for their success are not always present and are not easily achieved.[24]

In fact, we would say that the principle of nationality—cultural and linguistic nationalism in multinational states, particularly those with a dominant national culture and identity and without a clear territorial separation of the different communities—is not likely to lead to stable democracies. Perhaps constant renegotiation of the processes of assimilation that assure homogeneity of political subunits might allow the creation of a multinational state in which the basic sentiment would be one of loyalty to a state rather than a national identification.[25] Unfortunately, in the modern world the aim seems to be to build nations rather than states, a task that is probably beyond the capacity of any state that has not achieved the characteristics of a nation-state before the era of nationalism. In an age in which all national cultures or languages are in principle considered equal, in which all occupational roles are increasingly linked with the use of language in writing, and in which people increasingly live in large, heterogeneous urban centers in constant communication with public and private bureaucracies, mass media, etc., it is impossible to build a nation on the basis of cultural homogeneity. The federalists and advocates of regional or local community self-government would say that this is no major problem if the central authorities are ready to devolve many matters, if not most, to subunits. Without entering into the question of whether a modern industrial economy and state organization can function effectively and equitably with such decentralization, the problem remains unsolved if this devolution means only a transfer of the problem from a national level to a lower unit of government. Certainly, decentralization can make possible the coexistence of multiple nationalities within the territory of one state and avoid the permanent minority status of a particular group by making it the majority in its territory. The trouble starts when such a policy makes another group a permanent minority within that autonomous territory, as it frequently does. This is likely to be the case in most multinational states, since centuries of coexistence, internal migrations, assimilation to dominant culture, loss of cultural identity of important segments of the population, and the advantage of more powerful languages are likely to have destroyed the cultural homogeneity of the subunits. Furthermore, the processes of rapid economic development, industrialization, and the differentials in birthrate between the developed and less-developed regions are likely to produce large-scale internal migrations from the less-developed to the more highly developed parts of the country, further reducing the homogeneity of the sub-units. This inevitably means that in any subunit to which autonomy is granted there will be permanent minorities who will feel the same way about their status as the former minority felt in the national political unit. The democratic process with its civil liberties cannot itself guarantee, either de jure or de facto, the rights of such a minority against subtle discrimination and efforts at assimilation. If the majority is committed to increasing the national cultural homogeneity in its territory, and the minority is committed to retaining its distinctive cultural heritage, a large number of policy issues are likely to become sources of conflict. Prosperity permits certain solutions—the multi-plication of all public services in different languages, for example—but in a poor country some of those solutions are not available. In addition, as the sociolinguists have stressed, there is likely to be a ranking of the languages, a segregation of spheres of use, that ultimately implies an inequality that is likely to be intolerable for one or another group and will lead to efforts to redress the situation by political means.[26] A permanent minority of this type has no redress against a majority committed to its own values except appeal to the power of outside authorities, with the inevitable consequence of political and constitutional conflicts that will be extremely difficult to solve. If, in addition, that minority can call on the support of a power outside the state, its actions will be particularly threatening and will probably lead to legal and illegal actions incompatible with the free society. Secession, either to join another state or to transform the nation into a nation-state, is the likely con-sequence. The coexistence of different populations in the same territory, how-ever, is likely to leave the new state with the same heritage.

It is clear that democracy does not provide an easy answer to the question of under what conditions secession is legitimate, inevitable, and viable. Who is to define the territorial boundaries of the unit to secede, what sort of majorities are to be required, and what guarantees should be given to the remaining new minorities? Sometimes history provides boundaries in which the decision-making process can take place, but those historical borders are often far removed from the cultural and linguistic borders and the feelings of identity that have developed over time. Shall the units in which a majority for seces-sion should be allowed to carry the day be the whole region, provinces, municipalities, or neighborhoods? The larger the unit, the larger the number of minorities that will be tempted to secede from the new state; the smaller the unit used in making the decision democratically, the less likely it is that this newly emerging state will be viable in terms of geographic boundaries, eco-nomic resources, communications, and historical identity. What should be done about the geographical enclaves in the midst of the new state or in its large, heterogeneous cities that have resulted from assimilation and/or internal migrations? One answer has been the transfer and exchange of populations that has been done on a massive scale after wars of conquest and defeat in Eastern Europe and between Greece and Turkey after World War I. However, with minor exceptions, such transfers have been carried out without asking the people involved if they wanted to move or stay where they had always lived. It does not seem very democratic to impose such a decision by force even when it appears legitimate to make people choose. The realities of modern developing economies, however, are unlikely to allow large-scale relocation as a permanent solution, and commitment to the equality of languages and cultures is not likely to allow a policy of discrimination in favor of assimilation.

In a world rife with nationalism there are no easy solutions, and perhaps no solutions at all, to these dilemmas within the context of a liberal society. This accounts for the instability of the democracies in multinational states.[27] It also accounts for the likelihood that one or another group will turn to outside intervention to protect its interests, to the imposition by authoritarian regimes, or at best to the coordination of multinational units by an elite identified with a larger political unit and not responsive to nationalistic demands from the people. Any of those likely responses to the problems of a multinational state means the end of democracy, if democracy is taken to mean rule by the majority with respect for the rights of the minority and opportunities for the latter to participate in the decision-making process.

Even when the nationalistic sentiments of the majority do not favor such exclusivistic and ultimately secessionist solutions, the problem is far from easy to handle within the framework of a multinational democratic state. In such a state, even when it is supported by majorities, both in the subunit and the larger political unit, who are making reasonable compromises on policy issues, there are likely to be powerful minorities questioning, sometimes violently, any solution except full independence. There are likely to be other minorities ready to maintain the larger unit as a state or to engage in nation-building by assimilation and even force. Unfortunately, when such extremist minorities are repressed by one or another political unit, they are likely to find varying degrees of support even among those opposed to maximalist solutions, particularly when an effort is made to repress them as well. The interplay between a secessionist ultranationalist minority and moderate nationalist movements, accommodating parties at the center and extremist unitary parties at the center, imposes a heavy strain on a democratic state. The secessionist and the unitary centralist minorities have an easy target in the moderates at the periphery and at the center, and their attempts to find compromise solutions will be considered illegitimate, if not treasonable, by the extremists. That interaction is likely to be even more complicated when any of those four political alignments is divided by other issues like class or the religious-secularist cleavage, a division that is likely to occur in economically advanced countries. In that case, cooperation on the national question between the moderates at the center and those on the periphery, who take opposite sides on other issues, is likely to be difficult, and the temptation to collaborate with moderates and even extremists in the opposition in one or the other unit increases. This would be only natural for democratic political parties, but it acquires a different significance when a regional nationalist government of one political coloring allies itself with an opposition at the center, or the central government allies itself with a regional opposition supporting its demands against the regional government. In such a context, normal conflicts of interest and ideology acquire an additional intensity and meaning through interpretation either as secessionist threats or as an effort to undermine regional autonomy. Tempers are likely to flare, and normal constitutional conflicts may be perceived as threats to a regime, if not the state. The normal democratic mechanism of decision by shifting majorities is not likely to enjoy a particular legitimacy in such a context.

If we add appeals to neighboring countries sympathetic to the peripheral nationalisms for their own reasons—linguistic or ethnic affinity, or just plain power politics—the instability is likely to increase, and the predisposition to take repressive measures against minorities perceived as semi- or disloyal will be reinforced. Such measures are likely to intensify the tension. The presence of mixed populations with divided loyalties complicates the picture even further. Defense of their interests and their manipulation by the central government offers an opportunity to challenge the democratic representativeness of the regional government and parties.

It is no accident, therefore, that few multinational states have been stable democracies. This, in addition to many other factors, accounts for the lack of consolidation of Eastern European and Balkan democracies in the interwar years and those of many Third World countries outside Latin America after independence. Our decision to limit the cases to be included in this volume to relatively stable states that were, for most of their citizens, nation-states, does not allow us to pursue this complicated problem. The chapter on Spain provides some evidence of the contribution of multinationalism to the crisis of a democracy, although class and ideological conflicts were ultimately more decisive in that case. The ambiguity of statehood versus nation was, as Walter Simon has shown, one of the problems of the First Republic of Austria.[28] Even without a specifically nationalistic component, the conflicts between the Länder and the Reich in the Weimar Republic, particularly the rightist stronghold in Bavaria, and the memory of secessionist efforts after World War I, like those in Rhenania, contributed to the worsening of the political climate in Germany.[29] From this perspective it would have been very desirable to analyze the Czechoslovakian case as a combination of internal and external pressures endangering democratic stability; in fact, in view of such problems the relative stability of that new Central European democracy appears even more worthy of study from a theoretical point of view.

Crisis, the Democratic Party System, and Government Formation

Inability of the regime-sustaining forces to find solutions to pressing problems when faced with disloyal oppositions and increasing violence is reflected in government instability and growing difficulty in forming coalitions; in the fractionalization and subsequent fragmentation of parties; and in shifts in the electorate toward the extremes. These three processes tend to be interrelated and mutually reinforcing, and therefore the acts of the regime leaders aimed at preventing them can be essential steps in the process of reequilibration in the face of crisis.

The three processes often inaugurate a new phase, characterized by loss of power and a transfer of authority to ademocratic elements in the constitution. This is a result of the abdication of responsibility by democratic leaders and their growing dependence on the support of state structures that are more permanent or less immediately dependent on the electorate. Ultimately, the sequence of events is likely to lead to a reduction of the political arena and the growing influence of small, ill-defined groups. In these later phases different political forces begin to consider the possibility of coopting disloyal oppositions, as they are unable or unwilling to isolate and repress them.[30] In this stage even regime-supporting parties attempt to act semiloyally to the regime. This sequence of events that we have described is not inevitable, but becomes increasingly probable; it represents a downward road, a narrowing of alternatives, a funneling process that ultimately must be resolved by a change of regime or, in the best of cases, a solution within the regime.

Let us focus on the more immediate consequences of the crisis for the party system and its capacity to produce stable, efficacious governments and consequently to retain the loyalty of a sufficiently large segment of the electorate.

Problems that fit our characterization of being unsolvable put the government on the defensive. Parliamentary debates require increased attention, while other issues are likely to be neglected. Those members most responsible for policy failures are likely to resign. Latent tensions within and between government parties become explicit, and cabinet reorganization follows. Such problems may be more serious and visible in the case of multiparty coalition governments. Certain component members, particularly minor parties on the extremes of the spectrum within the coalition, begin to reconsider their commitment and explore alternative coalitions or a temporary withdrawal from responsibilities of government. The same would hold for one of the major parties if its interests and expectations were negatively affected. Concern for the electoral consequences of continuing in government might lead such parties to withdraw from direct governmental responsibility. Whenever the head of state has the constitutional power to dissolve parliament and call new elections, he faces a choice between a realignment of coalitions, a minority government of lowered efficiency, or dissolution.

What we have been describing is a normal process in parliamentary democracies, and the outcome might well be a realignment of forces within the spectrum of democratic parties as has occurred so often in the Third and Fourth French Republics and postwar Italy. The existence of a real political force in the center, with *Koalitionsfähigkeit* on both sides of the spectrum and sufficient parliamentary strength, can make it workable even for prolonged periods of time. It may lead, however, to limited efficacy of the system and internal erosion of the dominant Center party.[31]

For many reasons, the impossibility of such a solution in extremely fragmented, centrifugal, multiparty systems without elections on fixed dates leads to dissolution and a shift of the decision to the electorate. In societies where the parties have penetrated the whole electorate and created subcultures that allow only minor shifts of independent voters, and where there is widespread consensus that certain extremist parties constitute a disloyal opposition and should remain isolated, the outcome might not differ much from that of the elections preceding the crisis. In these situations the voters realize that there is no real alternative, and the appeal of the democratic parties is based on the rejection of both extremes more than on the accomplishments of the regime-supporting parties. The more or less minor realignments that result can keep the system going. The situation changes decisively, however, when the disloyal oppositions make considerable electoral gains. As a result, the system parties may feel that they should stay out of the government in order to be better able to compete with disloyal oppositions and to be free to join the opposition to the weakened government coalition.

If the cycle just described takes place several times in relatively rapid succession, without a reequilibration effort through formation of a regime-supporting coalition at the governmental or electoral level, a loss of efficacy and ultimately of the legitimacy of the regime may result. The last three years of the Weimar Republic exemplify this process, even though Hindenburg's electoral success, founded on the support of the democratic parties against the extremist candidates, indicated a certain potential for reequilibration. A good example of the opposite response to what might have become a regime crisis occurred in Belgium in 1936, when parties rallying behind Van Zeeland in a byelection caused a setback to the Rex party.[32]

The causes of extreme multipartism with centrifugal tendencies have been the subject of considerable study. Obviously, the complexity of the social structure and the multiple cleavages that result, the persistence of ideological traditions, and the divisive consequences of ideological politics are the main factors. A feeble electoral system, particularly one with pure proportional representation, exercises no restraint on the voters, and in the case of a feeble party system it furthers the persistence of fragmentation. In the case of a fragmented and polarized multiparty system with an electoral law that does not reward efforts at cooperation by the system parties, but fosters competition among them in addition to their activities against the disloyal oppositions, the calling of new elections is not likely to be of much help in solving the crisis. After all, electoral competition will probably bring out the differences in interests and ideological commitments of the regime-supporting parties, making their collaboration afterward even more difficult. Furthermore, by blaming the regime rather than a particular party, and by offering simplistic solutions that they will not be called upon to implement, the antisystem parties can benefit from the discontent of the electorate and make the system even more unworkable. They can ultimately achieve a negative majority that makes parliamentary government based on a majority principle almost impossible, and they can make governments dependent on the confidence of extra parliamentary powers. All the evidence points to the conclusion that in a crisis situation democratic parties are subject to very special strains that lead to fragmentation, withdrawal from responsibility, and mutual vetoes.

Fragmentation can become manifest in increased factionalism within parties that becomes visible at party congresses and leads to successive splits that increase the number of parties. The decisions necessary in a crisis situation force latent cleavages based on ideology, interest-group linkages, and personalities into the open. Crises impose decisions running counter to ideological commitments of the parties and sacrifices by closely linked interest groups, and they open up opportunities for struggles among leaders. Uncertainty about the reaction of a discontented electorate encourages such responses, as well as competition with neighboring parties, and creates among the leaders expectations of forming alternative coalitions. Even when this political fluidity might allow a disaggregated sequential solution of problems with shifting coalitions (as was the case in the Fourth Republic in France), it also creates in the public's mind an image of instability, lack of principle, dependence of parties on interest groups, opportunism, and struggle for personal power among leaders.

Events that would have a limited impact under normal circumstances serve to crystallize such tensions in crisis situations. Among them the historical record signals the importance of problems of public order and the indecisive or excessive responses to them by the agents of the government for which its leadership is made responsible; financial or personal scandals affecting the image of parties and leaders; the highly loaded issues of amnesty or execution of sentences, particularly death sentences, for political crimes; and the complex issues created by the division of power between executive, legislative, and judicial branches—in parliamentary systems, the relationship with the president or king. These problems in and of themselves might not be unsolvable in our sense, but they provide a dramatic scenario for the political rhetoric and moral indignation likely to divide the political class. To them we might add the suspicions created by alliances between leaders or parties with forces or institutions that can interfere with the political process, often called indirect powers, such as the church, the Vatican, Masonry, big business, high finance, and foreign powers.

Some readers may be surprised that our analysis does not deal with external intervention—overt or covert—in the breakdown process, particularly in view of the recent emphasis on this factor in the cases of Greece and Chile. In response to such criticism we would argue that without internal processes leading to a crisis of a regime, such interventions—short of military invasion— would not occur, much less be successful, in established nation-states. They might contribute to some extent to the final outcome, but they are not the cause of the crisis, nor are they likely to be the main variable in the process. Further- more, the classic cases, like the rise of Fascism to power, the breakdown of the Weimar Republic, and the events leading to the military uprising in Spain in 1936 (not the prolonged Civil War), were unrelated to any foreign intervention.

Abdication of Democratic Authenticity

One not infrequent consequence of the loss of cohesion in regime- supporting coalition parties is the effort to remove highly conflictive issues from the arena of partisan politics by transforming them into legal or technical questions. The aim is to gain time, since legal solutions are notoriously slow. Typically, questions of constitutionality are raised about certain laws and decisions, and issues are referred to constitutional courts. The legitimacy of having judicial bodies make what are essentially political decisions in a de- mocracy is always doubtful, and in countries where judicial bodies have been established only recently, their judgment is even less likely to be considered binding. Another device is to substitute experts and high-ranking civil ser- vants for representatives of the parties in politically exposed positions and to take refuge behind the technical nature of the decisions. Economic policy may be left in the hands of a presumably apolitical director of a central bank, and more and more cabinet posts are assigned to nonparty ministers or civil servants, allowing the politicians and the parties to avoid responsibility. Party leaders might participate in government as individuals without the mandate of their parties, which accordingly are not obliged to support their initiatives. The most powerful party leaders refuse to accept the prime ministership or to help form coalition governments. They delegate their responsibilities to second-level leaders, who are presumably ready to do their bidding, generally without independent authority or prestige, and are sometimes of limited ability.[33] The ambiguous relations between those second-level leaders and the men for whom they stand in, and their difficulties in communicating, plus the nurturing of their ambitions by other leaders, further complicate the political process. The result is a lessening of the authenticity of democratic institutions, particularly the power and responsibility of parliament.

In such situations the influence of the head of state, be it president or king, increases. He will be tempted to use his own judgment, which will lead to more government instability and often the calling of new elections. The growing influence of the head of state, the judiciary, the higher civil service, and sometimes the heads of the armed forces represents a shift of power from the democratically accountable leadership—a shift to what Carl Schmitt calls the neutral powers: nonpartisan, above party sources of authority—and with it the denaturation and loss of substance of the democratic process.[34]

In societies where important institutions—particularly the army, but also the civil service and other groups—feel a strong identification with a continuing center of authority identified as the "state" and distinct from the parties, these changes justify authoritarian tendencies. Rainer Lepsius, in his chapter, has shown how the possibility of interpreting Article 48 of the Weimar Constitution broadly facilitated the abdication of responsibility by the leading democratic parties, created the "impossible game" of presidential cabinets and emergency legislation, and encouraged ideological tendencies toward antidemocratic, authoritarian, bureaucratic rule consistent with the pre-1918 tradition. In Germany this solution proved too unstable to withstand a dynamic disloyal opposition led by a charismatic figure capable of rallying broad support for a silent revolution early in 1933.

A unique transition to authoritarian rule took place in Estonia and Latvia in the thirties. These were two of the smaller European democracies, born in 1918 on the border of the Soviet Union, close to Finland culturally, and oriented toward the West. Both had attained relatively homogeneous social structures after successful agrarian reforms, which reduced the initial radicalization of the Russian Revolution.[35] It was not the challengers of the extreme Right or the extreme Left who interrupted the normal functioning of their democratic institutions, nor was it the armed forces. Rather, it was the democratically elected leaders: President Päts in Estonia and President Ulmanis in Latvia. There seemed to be two main alternatives: instability with a democratic framework, due to the presence of important Fascist movements and governmental instability, due to the large number of small parties (multiplied, particularly by Latvia, by those representing ethnic minorities, and by proportional representation) and the impact of the world economic crisis; *or* an authoritarianism with roots outside the established political framework, which would probably have resulted in a Fascist regime. The leaders of the democratic parties, using the prestige they had gained during the struggle for independence, overcame the threat posed by a nonparliamentary right wing by establishing authoritarianism in order to thwart it. The last democratic cabinet, executing a bloodless palace coup, presided at the autodemise of democracy in 1934.

A particular case of abdication and loss of democratic authenticity, sometimes suffered in an effort to reequilibrate a system in crisis, is the effort by political leaders to seek the support of military command by offering cabinet posts or even the prime ministership to leading officers. This is a way of asking for an explicit pledge of support, but it indicates that the normal, implicit loyalty of the armed forces is in doubt. This will inevitably lead to a heightened politicization of the officer corps and will ultimately force it to decide whether it is willing to continue supporting the regime in the same way that a party gives support through the participation of its ministers in a coalition. This will heighten the internal ideological divisions within the officer corps and will ultimately force a decision about the legitimacy of the government, and perhaps the regime.[36]

Salvador Allende's decision to persuade the three armed forces chiefs to enter the cabinet in response to the crisis in the commercial supply system and the first truckers' strike is a good example. They defined their participation as nonpolitical, designed merely to defuse the situation and guarantee honest congressional elections. General Prats insisted that their presence be only temporary, since he felt it was "dangerous for the armed forces to appear linked to a government where ideologies are so defined." A majority of the officers opposed that political role which they felt compromised their professional character.

These processes are all more likely in a crisis situation, but in our view, they are not inevitable. They are generally chosen as temporary devices, as delaying actions, without full awareness of their long-term implications. Leaders of democratic parties who are ready to formulate policies and confront their followers with the real alternatives, to demand obedience and pose the question of confidence, to confront powerful interests even within their own constituency and overcome ideological rigidities and personal feuds, can gain a broad base of public support. Even at this stage the process of loss of authenticity of democracy is often a question of failure of leadership.

Excursus on Presidential and Parliamentary Democracies

Our emphasis on the role of "neutral" powers, based on the roles of King Victor Emmanuel and Hindenburg, but also of Shinfrud in Finland and Coty in France, rests on the European experience. Rereading our analysis, we realize that there is an obvious difference between parliamentary or semiparliamentary regimes like the Weimar Republic and presidential systems like the United States and the Latin American republics. The directly elected presidents, with their own democratic legitimacy and strong executive powers, who are free to appoint a cabinet that does not require a vote of confidence from the legislature, obviously occupy a totally different position in the political system. In a sense, the Reichspräsident in the Weimar constitution and the current French president occupy an intermediate and hybrid position.

Impressed by the stability of the paradigmatic presidentialist democracy in the United States, and the recurrent crises and critiques of parliamentarism, scholars have asked few questions about the relationship between these two major constitutional types of democracy and political stability. The almost automatic commitment to presidentialism within the Latin American constitutional tradition, and the more recent predominance of behavioralist sociological analyses of Latin American politics, has led to an almost total neglect of the role of presidentialism in political instability south of the Rio Grande. The earlier literature in particular is full of references to "caudillismo," "personalism," and "continuismo," but those phenomena are interpreted in historical and cultural terms rather than linked to institutional arrangements and constraints. The hispanic cultural tradition, the negative image of European, particularly French, parliamentarism held by Spanish-speaking intellectuals, and for a long time, their admiration for the United States constitution, did not encourage questions about the virtues of presidentialism. On the other hand, Americans, satisfied, on the whole, with their constitution, were not likely to attribute any share in the recurrent crises of most presidential regimes (which happen to be Ibero-American or African) to the institution of the presidency. This dual outlook is also reflected in the contributions to this volume.

However, when reviewing the cases included in our purview, a question came to mind: Does presidentialism have something to do with the political instability of Latin American democracies? The question was triggered in part by a comparison—admittedly a very superficial one—between Italy and Argentina. In both we find antisystem parties, the Communists and the Peronists, with relatively similar proportions of the vote (at least in the years following the fall of Perón). Both are linked with powerful trade unions and are distrusted by large sections of the society and by the Establishment, but the consequences of their presence have long been very different. It would be too much to say that the ideological distance between the Peronists and other parties and social groups was larger (at least until recently) than that between the PCI and the Christian Democrats or the Liberals, to say nothing of the neo-Fascists. Reading Guillermo O'Donnell's description in this volume of the "impossible game," particularly in the Frondizi period, one might ask oneself: Why has the Italian political game been less "impossible"?)

In answer, we might consider the following hypothesis. The presidential election "game" has a zero-sum character, whereas a parliamentary system offers the possibility of dividing the outcomes. Parliamentary elections present many options: formation of coalition governments; cooperation between government and opposition in the legislative process, either overtly or covertly; and the potential for gains by opposition parties in successive elections (particularly in centrifugal multiparty systems). This reduces the frustrations of the loser, creates expectations for the future, and often allows the loser a share in the power. In a presidential system, in which the winner of a plurality of 33.1 percent gains control of the executive office for a fixed period in time and dispenses relatively freely the power to appoint all high officers, to introduce legislation, and to veto the proposals of the legislature, the opposition is likely to feel impotent and even enraged. An opposition that was divided in the election has many reasons to come together after defeat; in turn, the incumbent is likely to fear frustration of his program and feel that at the end of his term he might well face defeat. The unipersonal magistracy, the plebiscitarian character of the election, and even the contrast between the national scope of issues debated in the presidential contest and the localism, clientelism, and possible corruption of legislative elections—all these factors are likely to give the president a sense of power, of having a mandate that is likely to exceed his real support, and will exacerbate his irritation when he is faced with a legislature unwilling to respond to his leadership. Some of the factors we have just mentioned were certainly present in the crises of Brazil under Goulart and Chile under Allende.

"But why not in the United States?" one might ask. However, we should not forget the fragmentation of the U.S. political arena between federal and state governments, the strong institutional position of the Supreme Court, the prestige of the Senate, and—a factor often ignored—the bipartisan recruitment of many officials (including the Cabinet) and the bipartisan formulation of certain policies in the United States. After all, political scientists have called for "responsible party government" because, to a large extent, American government is not party government.

In the case of polarization of ideology or interest, the zero-sum character of the presidential game undoubtedly introduces pressures to limit its consequences: no reelection, the attempt of the legislature to veto or filibuster the decision-making process, efforts to use the courts to limit the power of the president, the resistance of state governments (particularly when headed by powerful governors who are popularly elected and belong to a different party), often even the separate election of presidents and vice presidents of different parties or coalition, and finally, the intervention of the armed forces as "poder moderador." All those devices lead to constitutional conflicts that weaken the system, endanger its legitimacy, and frustrate presidents who feel that they have a direct, popular, plebiscitarian mandate. (Of course, this mandate is often only a plurality that in a parliamentary regime would oblige them to work with the opposition or act as a "tolerated" minority government.) On the other hand, a large segment of the electorate, identified with a popular president, understanding little about all those maneuvers or legal constitutional battles, is likely to feel frustrated by those it perceives as a "minority" identified with vested interests. In view of all this, even when the ideological distance between supporters of a president and his opposition might be the same or smaller than the distance between government parties and the opposition in a parliamentary system, the conflict might be more intense.

Another difference between presidential and parliamentary systems, be they constitutional monarchies or republics, is that there is—with the exception of the courts, who are often weak—no moderating power. A king or president in Europe can respond to a change in the constellation of political forces in parliament; the power of dissolution or the threat of its use can lead to a restructuring of the government in a critical situation; and a government leader who has failed can generally be replaced, with his cooperation. A president, in contrast, is elected for a fixed period, and his ouster involves a constitutional crisis. This helps to explain why the military frequently assume the "moderating" function. They are often encouraged by a frustrated opposition and feel "legitimated" by constitutional provisions making them the defenders of the constitution.

The differences we have noted may contribute to an understanding of why there were a number of transitions from democracy to nondemocratic rule in Europe that took place semi- or pseudo-constitutionally, and even at the time were not perceived as a break in democratic legitimacy. Let us not forget how many observers viewed the advent of Mussolini to the premiership. A manifesto of the Partito Communista Italiano issued on 28 October (*L'Ordine Nuovo*, 29 October)—a day before the arrival of Mussolini in Rome as premier designate—reaffirmed the equivalence of the Fascist and a democratic solution. Two days later, *Rassegna Communista* wrote: "We deny that the coming to power has any revolutionary character or any remote similarity to a coup d'état. . . . A coup d'état overthrows one leading class and changes the fundamental laws of a state; until today the Fascist victory has renewed the cabinet." Nenni, the Socialist leader, reminiscing in 1964, wrote: "Everyone in Italy agreed in not taking Fascism seriously."

In the case of presidential regimes, such a *Machtübergabe*—like those in Germany and Austria at the end of World War I, the appointments of Mussolini and Hitler, or the change from a Labour government to a National government under MacDonald—would not have been possible. To change the government in a presidential regime when the president is unwilling—and few are likely to be willing to relinquish the office—requires a break with the rules of democratic election of the chief executive: government crises almost by definition become regime crises. And although some political scientists might be ready to say that military intervention of the "poder moderador" is the functional alternative to reshuffling a parliamentary coalition, the two are not equivalent in terms of democratic legitimacy and the stability and legitimation of institutions of popular government.

In view of these considerations, perhaps the consequences of the "presidential" versus the "parliamentary" game in democracies deserves further and more systematic analysis.

4.

The End
of Democracy

Loss of Power, Power Vacuum, and the Preparation for a Transfer of Power or Confrontation

Unsolvable problems, a disloyal opposition ready to exploit them to challenge the regime, the decay of democratic authenticity among the regime-supporting parties, and the loss of efficacy, effectiveness (particularly in the face of violence), and ultimately of legitimacy, lead to a generalized atmosphere of tension, a widespread feeling that something has to be done, which is reflected in heightened politicization. This phase is characterized by the widespread circulation of rumors, increased mobilization in the streets, both anomic and organized violence, toleration or justification of some of those acts by some sectors of society, and above all, increased pressure from the disloyal opposition. The readiness to believe in conspiracies and the rapid diffusion of rumors, sometimes encouraged by limits imposed on the news media in an attempt to control the situation, contribute to the uncertainty and unpredictability that may lead to worsening of economic crises.

In this atmosphere the leading actors may decide not to confront the basic problems of the government but to try to overcome the political crisis. Typically, efforts are made to strengthen the power of the executive, sometimes by proposing constitutional amendments, granting emergency powers, suspending the sessions of the legislature, intervening, suspending, or interfering with regional or local governments, or reshuffling the top-level military command. If such measures were combined with a growing cohesion of the regime-supporting parties, a clear assumption of responsibility by their most outstanding leaders, a capacity and willingness to maintain order without bias in favor of those closer to the parties in power, and rejection of any collaboration with a disloyal opposition, they might lead to a reequilibration process.

A second alternative would be an attempt to expand the bases of the regime by incorporating at least part of the disloyal opposition or coopting its leadership for a new coalition. As we shall see, this leads at best to a transformation of the regime, and more often to a transfer of power, a *Machtübergabe*, which the disloyal opposition might transform quickly into a *Machtübernahme*. This

75

was the case in Italy in 1922, Germany in 1933, and Czechoslovakia in 1948.

/A third alternative would be to allow the process of polarization to continue and ignore the threats coming from disloyal oppositions and semiloyal elements in a pre–civil war situation until one of the disloyal forces attempts to assume power. The democratic leadership then has only two options: to withdraw, turning over its power to the armed forces, sometimes under the cover of apolitical institutions like the supreme court, in the hope that the moderating power will not introduce a regime change but will only suspend normal democratic processes temporarily; or to appeal to the nation and to mobilize organized forces (like the trade unions), including those considered disloyal or semiloyal, in an effort to broaden its authority. In a highly polarized society this second option (taken by the Spanish minority bourgeois Republican government after it failed to reach a compromise with a military pronunciamento) means civil war. Only with a rapid victory could the government continue to claim democratic legitimacy rather than become the legitimizer of a revolutionary transformation of the regime or proceed with the transfer of power. French politicians, particularly Guy Mollet, were certainly aware of these possibilities in May 1958 when they rejected the chance to resist the military coup in Algiers by appealing to mass mobilization in which the Communists would have played a leading role.[1] They were haunted by the memory of the Spanish government in July 1936 and its dependence on the militias of the proletarian revolutionary parties, particularly the Anarcho-Syndicalists and the maximalist Socialists.

In a society in which the democratic leadership has experienced such a loss of power, if the army is not apt to assume the role of a moderating power and the disloyal oppositions convey ambiguous signals that combine a willingness to participate in a solution with the capacity to present a revolutionary threat, the pattern of transfer of power is the most likely. In fact, it might appear to be the best possible solution, should the neutral powers provide it with a stamp of legitimacy, the armed forces tolerate or even welcome it, and at least some of the regime-supporting parties believe that they have enough bargaining power to protect their interests and certain institutional arrangements.

Legal revolution was first attempted in the defeated states after World War I and opened the door to the establishment of democratic republics in Germany and Austria.[2] Mussolini, however, perfected the process in favor of a disloyal opposition and an antidemocratic regime. After the failure of the Beer Hall Putsch, Hitler realized that power could be gained only with the appearance of legality, and in 1933 he succeeded in much less time than the Italian Fascists. Although there are undeniable differences, the 1948 coup in Prague shows some similarities. The situation in late May 1958 in Paris again showed some similarities, even though the unique personality of de Gaulle and his commitment to democracy changed what appeared to be a threat to a democratic regime into a transformation that can be considered a reequilibration of democracy as well. Since the process of "legal" takeover was so successful in those cases, analysis seems relevant even when the historical record makes it difficult to apply the same formula today. We might note that legal revolution—using constitutional institutions against their clear intent or what the Germans would call *verfassungswidrige Verfassungsänderung*—has been used by the Suárez government in Spain (1976–77) to make possible the transition from an authoritarian regime to democracy. In this case, the pressure brought to bear by the opposition, its mobilization of the street, and the rising cost of repression convinced the rulers to inaugurate the transition to democracy. They did this without coopting the opposition leaders into the government, and without a breakdown of the institutional framework (*ruptura*), but with a clear discontinuity.

This situation occurs when a democratic regime that has experienced a serious loss of power and legitimacy is confronted with a disloyal opposition possessing considerable striking power due to its capacity for mass mobilization and its readiness to use the threat of force, but also due to its presence in parliament which enables it to facilitate a formal constitutionally legal assumption of power with the cooperation of other parties. A disloyal opposition that has gained power bases through mobilizing the streets and employing organized paramilitary groups, but whose leader is prepared to talk sensibly and to declare, albeit ambiguously, his readiness to respect at least some key institutions and to moderate his extremist supporters, if granted a share in power, finds itself in the best position for a takeover. Opportunistic concessions to a variety of interests and institutions are aimed at neutralizing their opposition to the entry into the government. Perhaps the ability to control a heterogeneous following and the absence of lieutenants who might question the compromises being made on the road to power is another condition for the success of this tactic. It was certainly a decisive asset to Hitler that none of his opponents in the NSDAP could command any following in the party.

To succeed, however, this tactic requires certain responses both on the part of some of the parties and leaders not previously linked with the disloyal opposition and on the part of the neutral powers of the state. The process of formally legal or semilegal takeover is initiated when some of the parties or leaders who are far from committed to an overthrow of democracy feel that the antiregime leadership could be coopted without danger to the system or at the cost of such transformations as a strengthened executive, the outlawing of a party, or the curtailment of some civil liberties. Their actions tend to be based on the assumption that they might be senior partners in the new coalition, as was the case when von Papen thought that he had engaged Hitler, rather than the other way around. At one point or another, leaders of the regime may agree with some of the objectives of the disloyal opposition, if not its methods, and will be tempted to explore the conditions under which they might reach an agreement that would bring the disloyal opposition, or a sector of it, into the system. One obvious strategy is an attempt to split the disloyal opposition, as when Schleicher dreamed of exploiting the divergence between Strasser and Hitler.

Arguments for this action are as follows: the leader might be more amenable to compromise than many of his followers; a share in responsibility will moderate extremist positions; participation in power will stop unmanageable street violence; and cooptation will effect suppression of another disloyal opposition perceived as more dangerous. These hopes are encouraged by the ambiguous statements of the disloyal opposition's leader and seem to be confirmed by internal tensions within his own movement. The initiatives for such negotiations are often handled by intermediaries who have their own reasons for favoring such a solution; they tend to be taken in secret and are broken off when they become public. At this stage regime-supporting parties or factions in them and individual leaders move into positions we might call semiloyal. Often the neutral powers look favorably on such a solution, or at least, careful of their own survival, do not reject it outright. The result is a growing atmosphere of suspicion in the political class that often leads to further fragmentation within the parties, including the disloyal opposition itself, and provokes the accusation that the leadership is ready to sell out the movement, its more radical goals, and its leaders for a cabinet post. This accelerates the pace of events toward denouement.[3]

Secret negotiations, the need to get the approval of the neutral powers, the benevolent neutrality of the armed forces, and the desire of interest groups to solve the crisis are all factors leading to a transfer of the political process from the parliamentary arena to another, invisible and much more restricted. The narrowing of the arena and the important role played by small groups of individuals is characteristic of this final phase in the process of breakdown. (By a strange coincidence, as Daniel Bell has pointed out, these groups— conspiracies, clubs, committees, cabals, courts, *camarillas,* caucuses—all begin with a small "c.") Their presence explains why the breakdown process has been so often analyzed in terms of a conspiracy theory. These groups may have an important role in the immediate process of transfer of power, but they are a product of the entire process.

Another consequence of this slow, but mounting, exploration of an opening to the disloyal opposition is that the more important and permanent institutions of society begin to realize that extremists, formerly regarded with hostility or at least considerable ambivalence, might come into power.[4] Consequently, these institutions slowly but perceptibly disengage from the democratic regime and from those parties to whom they had entrusted their political interests. Typically, business organizations will begin to contribute to such parties; the churches will lift their injunctions against supporting or joining such parties and tend to become less identified with a religious party like the Populari or the Zentrum; the trade unions might reconsider their ties with political parties like the Social Democrats; and the army will insist on its loyalty to the state and its leader with the implicit message that its loyalty is not to a particular government or regime.[5] The leaders of a disloyal opposition will, of course, encourage these trends by an adroit use of expressions of respect for the institutions, specific promises and guarantees, and more or less veiled threats to prevent institutions from casting their lot with the existing regime.

The less politically committed segments of the population also begin to accept cooptation of the disloyal opposition, in the hope that it will lead to a more stable government, greater efficacy, and above all, an end to the politically inspired violence that they suffer as bystanders. Paradoxically, a disloyal opposition that has been a major contributor to the atmosphere of civil disorder can appear at this stage as offering a chance for order. This weakens the capacity of the more militant, prodemocratic forces to mobilize their supporters against their opponents' entry into the government, since at that stage they might be blamed for the outbreak of violence and civil war.

The discovery of what the Nazis would call legal revolution has increased the difficulty of bringing into the regime members of any opposition whose loyalty to the democratic system is suspect. Offering cabinet seats to representatives of such a party, which allows it to overcome the last threshold on the road to full legitimacy as a participant in democratic politics, might lead to an escalation of demands, bolstered by such pressures as well-orchestrated mass support on the streets. A slight shift in control of the state's power of coercion toward legitimating the actions of party militias could spell the inevitable doom of democracy.

But *Machtergreifung* and the subsequent consolidation of authoritarian or totalitarian rule is not the only threat to democracy in this case. The entry into the government of a party perceived by a large sector of the population or by key institutions like the army as semiloyal or disloyal to the institutions, even when it is not intent on a takeover, is likely to produce an "anticipated" reaction in the form of revolutionary protest, legitimized as the defense of democracy or a preventive military putsch. This was the case in Spain in 1934, when the CEDA's entry into the government served to justify the Asturian proletarian revolution, the secessionist putsch by the Catalan Generalitat government, and the withdrawal from participation in the institutions by the liberal Left bourgeois parties. Democracy managed to survive, but it had been mortally wounded. We must emphasize that macrohistorical political models of processes like the power takeovers by Mussolini and Hitler are never repeated according to the same script, largely because the participants in new but similar situations are likely to take into account, rightly or wrongly, what they think are the lessons of the past. In fact, it is surprising that some of the patterns are nevertheless repeated in macrosociological processes. For this reason model-building is not so feasible in macrosociology as in microsociology.

The model of the legal conquest of power—revolution from the top—

makes the Communist party's transition from negative integration to full participation in a democracy much more risky and difficult than that of the Socialist labor parties in the early decades of this century. The moral stance of early revolutionary movements did not allow their members to participate in government unless they constituted the democratically elected majority. When they did accept participation, it was under the assumption that this would help them build such a majority rather than use power to subvert the system. They would have rejected as immoral such a statement as: "The Constitution prescribes only the arena of the struggle; it does not specify the goal. We shall enter the legitimate organizations and in this way make our party the decisive factor. Once we possess the constitutional right to do so, we shall, of course, cast the state in the mold that we consider to be the right one"[6]—even if that mold required a change of regime. When democratic Socialists first entered democratic government, they did not expect (as rereading Harold Laski would show) that their opponents would allow them to pursue their policies legally.[7] In many cases they were wrong. But the fact that they were sometimes right gave new life to the maximalist interpretation of the Marxist heritage, a position well expressed in this text:

This permits us to do what the Third International [then] does not allow. That is to participate in a government with the Republicans and still recognize the transitory revolutionary dictatorship of the proletariat as the ineluctable postulate of scientific socialism.

What did the bourgeois newspapers suppose? Undoubtedly they supposed us to be inoffensive social democrats, full of pseudo-democratic prejudices, and so foolish that if it were necessary to prevent a fascist dictatorship, we would merely ask for new elections.[8]

The ambiguity of this position has had fateful consequences for democracy in many countries: Italy, Austria, Spain, and Chile.

The questions we have just raised are not academic when we consider the possibility of the participation of Italian and French Communists in government and their role in the Portuguese developments in 1975.

The End of a Democratic Regime and Its Aftermath

The death of a democracy is often recorded in the history books as associated with the date of a particular event: the March on Rome, Hitler's appointment as chancellor, the outbreak of the Spanish civil war, the attack on La Moneda and the death of Allende. But in fact, those fateful days or hours preceding the events that marked the end of a regime were only the culmination of a long and complex process. When they occurred, many of the actors probably did not realize or intend the fateful consequences. In many cases, the nature of the regime being born in such moments was not known even to those whose intent was to overthrow the existing political order. The transition to a new regime was often possible only because so many of the participants were unaware of the ultimate implications of their actions and, even more often, were mistaken in their analysis of the situation. In retrospect, it is possible to identify points at which opportunities existed for alternative courses of action that might have reduced the probability of the fall of the regime.

At the latter stages of the process that leads from the loss of power to the power vacuum, the question of the timing of decisions and actions becomes particularly relevant. The responses of the rulers and participants can be characterized (unfortunately, more often than not, *a posteriori*) as premature, timely, delayed, "eleventh-hour," or taken when time has run out. Reequilibration would require timely actions, while extrapolation from other crises might lead to premature responses that would accelerate rather than halt the breakdown. (The October revolution in Spain may be seen in this light.) But most examples are of belated actions (like those of the reformist Socialists of Turati in the Italian crisis of the twenties). The intellectual value of our analysis should consist, therefore, in that it should enable leaders of democracies facing serious crisis to be more conscious of the choices and risks they face.

One might wonder whether analysis of the circumstances of the final dénouement, while relatively uninteresting from the point of view of accounting for the death of democracy, might not be of great importance in understanding the nature of the regime that is emerging: its process of consolidation, its future stability, the possibilities of its transformation, its effect on the future of the society.

Depending on that transition, the difficulties and opportunities for the reestablishment of democracy are in some measure the result of that final stage of breakdown process and perhaps of the interpretations that the society and different actors give to those dramatic events. The end of a democratic regime, even when it can be dated symbolically, is also the beginning of the building of a new regime, a process that we see as having distinctive problems and patterns that require descriptive models.

We have focused on cases in which it was not possible in the final stage for those committed to the survival of democracy to prevent its demise. However, their options in that stage have decisive consequences for how the challengers of the democratic order can and will act. Certainly the end of a democracy shows a number of different patterns that deserve further research. The main patterns seem to be:

1. An unconstitutional displacement of a democratically elected government by a group ready to use force, whose action is legitimated by institutional mechanisms planned for emergency situations. Interim rule is set up

with the intent to reestablish the democratic process with certain deviations at a later time.

2. The assumption of power by a combination of ademocratic, generally predemocratic, authority structures that coopt part of the political class of the previous democratic regime and integrate elements of the disloyal opposition, but undertake only limited changes in the social structure and most institutional realms.

3. The establishment of a new authoritarian regime, based on a realignment of social forces and the exclusion of all the leading political actors of the preceding democratic regime, without, however, creating new political institutions or any form of mass mobilization in support of its rule.

4. The takeover of power by a well-organized disloyal opposition with a mass base in the society, committed to the creation of new political and social order, and unwilling to share its power with members of the political class of the past regime, except as minor partners in a transition phase. The outcome may range from the establishment of a self-confident authoritarian regime to a pretotalitarian regime.

5. The takeover of power that does not succeed even against a weakened regime and requires a prolonged struggle (civil war). Such a conflict can be the result of one of two variables, or more likely a combination of them: the willingness of the democratic government to resist the pressures to relinquish power by demanding the obedience of the coercive instruments of the state and the support of the population, combined with the inability to defeat its opponents; and the existence in the society of a high level of political and social mobilization, which may or may not be with the democratic government but is ready to challenge the takeover by its opponents.

The first of these five patterns was the traditional model of military intervention, the *poder moderador*, in nineteenth century Spain and Latin America. It was only possible in societies with relatively low levels of political mobilization, parties that were the personal following of leaders or coalitions of notables or caciques, and an army without its own political aims. Given the corruption of the electoral process under oligarchic democracy, and the readiness of large segments of the political class to encourage or accept such interventions, the result for the society was not too different from a rigged election replacing one group of politicians with another group similar in social composition and aims. Since the democracies fitting our definition (and studied in this volume) were, or were beginning to be, a different type, even when some of the participants in the military coups conceived their role in these terms and some of the politicians encouraged them to play the old role of the moderating power, the outcome was closer to the second and third patterns.

The second pattern would be the model of the transition to royal dictatorships in a number of Balkan countries. Rumania under King Carol and Yugoslavia in the interwar years provide interesting examples. The residues of traditional or semitraditional monarchical legitimacy for the army and some sectors of the population, combined with the problems of unsuccessful democratic regimes and conflicts between nationalities, make authoritarian regimes of a military-bureaucratic character possible. These regimes coopt large numbers of professional politicians who had been elected thanks to their local bases of power or the influence they were able to exercise by using the access to government. Semi- or pseudodemocratic mechanisms could be maintained by excluding minor activist groups ready to challenge the social or political order from political life and ignoring the demands of nationalities challenging the privileged status of a dominant nationality. The alternative to a "halfway" democracy was a semiauthoritarian regime, in which the main difference was loss of freedom for an opposition whose chances of gaining power democratically were already limited, but whose freedom might in the long run have represented a threat.

The breakdown of a democracy that has gained considerable legitimacy, whose parties have roots in the society representing various interests and distinctive ideologies, and whose leaders enjoy considerable appeal, is more likely to lead to the final three patterns, which represent a greater discontinuity and a real change of regime. Of these, the fourth on our list is unlikely to be the most frequent, since a disloyal mass political movement only rarely gains power in a democracy as the Fascists did in Italy and Germany. The unique circumstances that allowed such mass movements to challenge the state's monopoly of armed force combined with electoral successes and, aided by semiloyalty of other political forces and the neutrality of the armed forces, to proceed to a pseudolegal transfer of power without encountering popular resistance, are unlikely to be repeated in modern societies. Fascism as a mass movement, with its ideology, style, organizational inventiveness, and heterogeneous social basis, was a result of a unique historical situation after World War I.[9] Conservative interests, frightened by the Russian Revolution and local pseudorevolutions or revolutionary rhetoric, looked upon the Fascists as potential allies. The democratic liberal leaders, particularly in Italy, did not perceive the serious threat to their position that the new movement represented. Today they are not likely to put their hope for a defense against the threat of possible leftist revolution in an antidemocratic mass movement that could easily provoke a civil war. They will make a greater effort to work within the democratic framework, using the coercive resources of the state to defend it against radical challenges, confident that their interests can be protected within it, in the knowledge that the opponents on the left are not too likely to win power electorally and are unable to take it by force. Should they come to the conclusion that democracy does not guarantee an acceptable social order, they are more likely to turn to a preventive coup by the armed forces, with considerable active or passive support from the sectors of society being threatened. The outcome then would be an authoritarian regime with many of the characteristics of Fascist regimes, but bureaucratic-technocratic in nature, not based on the mass mobilization that precedes the breakdown of democracy. If the leaders were unsuccessful, the result would be a civil war whose outcome would be decided largely by military means and probable international intervention.

In spite of the high level of politicization of society, the mobilization of the masses, and the polarization that preceded the breakdown of a number of democracies, the takeover of power in a number of cases was not particularly bloody, even when the subsequent terror and repression of opponents were as great as they were in Germany. Breakdown leading to a real civil war has been the exception; undoubtedly, the pattern of legal revolution invented by Mussolini was unexpected and poorly understood, so that the Left was unable to initiate the sort of violent reaction that might have led to a civil war. Defeat without struggle was abetted by the Communist interpretation of Fascism in the interwar years: it was seen as a temporary phenomenon that would exhaust itself as the last stand of monopolistic capitalism revealed its failure to the masses and led to their disillusionment with social democracy, particularly when Moscow was advocating the theory of social Fascism.[10] The semilegal takeover of power, made possible by the semiloyal opposition legitimized by the neutral powers, the coerced decision of democratic parties, and the benevolent neutrality of the armed forces, together with the self-deception of many leaders about the consequences of the *Machtergreifung*, made any reaction impossible until it became too late to challenge the rapidly consolidating power of the Nazi state. The pattern was not to be repeated.

In Austria, a less threatening authoritarian alternative required a short civil war to consolidate itself in power, and in Spain, a few months later, a misperceived comparable situation led to the October revolution. In the middle thirties the situation had changed; democrats of various persuasions were more ready to cooperate to save democratic regimes against the Fascist danger; the Communists, after considerable hesitation, changed their line toward Socialist parties. In relatively stable societies the revolutionary rhetoric that had pushed many potential democrats into the arms of Fascism was abandoned, and conservatives were probably less enthusiastic about the Fascist mass movement. Only in Spain did a crisis of democracy, coming after its defeat in so many countries, produce a militant response by both the democrats and the proletariat. Both groups saw their gains threatened and at the same time saw an opportunity for revolution when the authority of the state was challenged by the army and its supporters on the right. Since the government felt confident of its democratic legitimacy and enjoyed the support of important sectors of the population, even among the army, police, and civil servants (a fact that is often ignored), it decided to resist the military uprising. Simultaneously, the working class, which had been organized for revolution, or at least organized to exercise pseudorevolutionary pressures on the government, was ready to respond to the threat and the appeal of the government. The loyalty, or at least the ambivalence, of some segments of the army, the mobilization of the masses by the proletarian organizations, and the hostility of regional nationalists to a centralist Right created resistance to the army and its civilian supporters in many parts of Spain. In other parts of the country, action by the military could mobilize widespread civilian support, making a quick defeat of the rebels by the loyalists impossible and therefore making a civil war, prolonged by foreign intervention, inevitable. The two political systems that fought each other for almost three years ended having little in common with the one existing in July 1936, and even less with the one established in 1931.

Although the model of the rise to power of a Mussolini or a Hitler will not be repeated, the possibility of the combined resistance of a democratic government with a leftist orientation and a mobilized working class, as in Spain, cannot be ignored in contemporary democracies. Unfortunately those who expect to combine democratic rule with rapid social and economic change, a combination perceived by both its supporters and its opponents as revolutionary, seem unlikely to succeed without a civil war if their opponents can gain the support of the armed forces. Even if the loyalists were to win, it would be a considerable time after a civil war before a government could function as a democracy, granting to the defeated the same political rights as the victors. Civil war, whatever the outcome, means the death of democracy and the establishment of some type of dictatorship.

Contrary to the beliefs and hopes of democrats, a democratic regime should never be allowed to approach the point at which its survival will depend on the readiness of its supporters to fight for it in the streets. Few citizens, even in a crisis, are ready to support those who might want to overthrow democracy, but in a modern society they feel unable to do anything in such a situation.[11] Only those on the extremes of the political spectrum are prepared to fight or are likely to have the organizational resources to do so. To resist the disloyalty of minorities, a democratic government must prevent their access to the means of violence by keeping them disarmed and politically isolated from mass support. Should such minorities be able to gain support from the levels of power that would allow them to command the loyalty or neutrality of the instruments of coercion of the state, the fate of the regime is in serious danger. A primary requirement of a stable democratic regime is retention of its legitimacy among those in direct control of the instruments of coercion. Any policy that would so deeply alienate them that they would be willing to rebel is not viable. In certain respect the armed forces in a modern society are a concurrent minority, in the sense that Calhoun uses the term. However, a government that enjoys legitimacy beyond its own electoral support is unlikely to encounter the disloyalty of more than a sector of the armed forces in a modern democracy. Its chances of survival depend on the response to its claim of legitimacy by those officers who are not committed to a coup. The loyalty of conscripts as citizens, the population irrespective of party in that context, and the mobilization of those committed to partial political goals (including those who for other reasons have questioned democracy's legitimacy) might not produce the most efficient response, and might in fact be counterproductive. Perhaps the only hope for a regime so threatened is to compromise with the insurgents, if they are too strong, or to seek the support of the armed forces not involved in the pronunciamento; that is, they should turn to certain organized sectors of the society rather than hope to defeat the insurgents by "arming the people." This solution, even at the cost of changes in policy, institutional changes, the curtailment of some civil liberties, or the cooptation of some semiloyal leaders, offers more hope for the future of democracy than do resistance and civil war. These considerations and the availability of the charisma of de Gaulle, who won considerable legitimacy far beyond his own partisan support, allowed the democratic leadership of the Fourth Republic to make the transition to the Fifth—a rare case of reequilibration.

Reequilibration can be the outcome of near-breakdown in a democratic regime. Unfortunately, few of the crises of democracy have been studied from this perspective. In fact, it could be argued that several of the democracies that ultimately failed had overcome previous crises, and that scholars should therefore place more emphasis on the positive aspects of the way those crises were surmounted.[12]

5.
The Process of Reequilibration

Reequilibration of Democratic Systems as a Problem

Reequilibration of a democracy is a political process that, after a crisis that has seriously threatened the continuity and stability of the basic democratic political mechanisms, results in their continued existence at the same or higher levels of democratic legitimacy, efficacy, and effectiveness.[1] It assumes a severe jolting of those institutions, a loss of either effectiveness or efficacy, and probably legitimacy, that produces a temporary breakdown of the authority of the regime. Reequilibration is compatible with changes of regime within the genus *democratic* (broadly defined); that is, it includes changes like those from the Fourth to the Fifth French Republic, or from a *régime censitaire* to modern mass democracy, or from a system based on majority rule to one based on consociational mechanisms. Reequilibration can be, even when it does not need to be, a breakdown or profound transformation of one regime, but not of democratic legitimacy and basic institutions.

Breakdown followed by reequilibration of democracy can be effected by anti- or aconstitutional means, by the interference in the normal democratic processes of a political actor (like a charismatic leader) whose initial legitimation is ademocratic, or by the use of force, as in a military putsch. Reequilibration, therefore, might be accompanied by a disjunction between what the German political scientists of the twenties called "legality" and "legitimacy." The new regime might be established illegally, but it must be legitimated by the democratic process afterward, and above all, it must operate thereafter according to democratic rules. It undoubtedly represents a violation of the condition of regime continuity, the continuous functioning of the established rules, and the mechanisms institutionalized to change them. In this sense de Gaulle's ascent to power in 1958 is unlike a change of government from Conservative to Labor in the United Kingdom or even Nixon's succession by Ford after impeachment proceedings started. The question we ask and will answer hypothetically at this point is, "Under what conditions is a reequilibration possible?"

The first condition would seem to be the availability of a leadership uncompromised by the loss of efficacy and legitimacy of the existing regime in crisis and committed to the creation of a new regime with new institutions to be

87

legitimated by future democratic procedures. Secondly, that leadership must be able to gain the acceptance of those who remained loyal to the existing regime as well as those who opted for disloyalty in crisis and therefore are potential supporters of a nondemocratic regime. Third, the leadership of the regime that has lost power, efficacy, effectiveness, and probably considerable legitimacy must be able to accept that fact and facilitate rather than oppose the transfer of power. Closely related to this requirement is the willingness of the former leadership, with its commitment to certain policy goals, ideologies, and interests, to subordinate the realization of these goals in order to save the substance of democracy, even at the cost of temporary discontinuity. Such willingness and ability presuppose confidence in the democratic commitment of the leadership to whom power will be transferred. Since no regime and its leadership are likely to have lost all their authority and legitimacy, the temptation and justification to resist illegal challenge exists. But as their opponents can also have a powerful claim to legitimacy, the outcome can only be the establishment of authoritarian rule or civil war, if that opposing claim is used to mobilize a sector of the population to resist the transfer of power and transformation of the regime. At a somewhat different level of significance, there is a fifth condition: a certain level of indifference and passivity in the bulk of the population must exist during the final denouement of the crisis. Furthermore, the reequilibration model is only possible when the semiloyal opposition to a particular regime is capable of controlling and neutralizing a disloyal opposition that questions not only the particular regime or government but the democratic system. It is a game in which the semiloyal actors in one regime consciously deceive the disloyal political forces whose challenge may have precipitated the breakdown and brought them to power.

The requirements of reequilibration would seem to be a unique constellation of factors. Reequilibration originates in a leadership outside of the regime in crisis but acceptable to many of its supporters; at the same time, this leadership is capable of bringing into a new regime many of its challengers and isolating diehard opponents. It is also committed to legitimizing the new regime by democratic means and continuing afterward with democratic institutions. Reequilibration occurs in the presence of the readiness of the electorate to approve the regime transformation or change, an approval conditioned by trust in the new regime's capacity to solve the unsolvable problem that precipitated the final crisis. These are requirements aptly fulfilled by the transition from the Fourth to the Fifth French Republic. De Gaulle's availability, his personal charismatic legitimacy, his commitment to democracy as he understood it, and the willingness of leading political figures of the Fourth Republic to cooperate, as well as the passivity of most of the metropolitan population of France in the crisis days, made it possible.[2] Low-keyed mobilization by the Communist party, facilitated by the unwillingness of most democratic leaders to counter the threat on the right by asking for Communist support, was another factor.

Albert Hirschman considers the problem of recuperation of a firm or organization whose performance has lapsed, and calls attention to some of the same requisites we have noted for the reequilibration process.[3] When he writes that it is generally best for a firm to have a mixture of *alert* and *inert* customers—alert ones to provide the firm with a feedback mechanism which starts the effort at recuperation, and inert customers to provide it with the time and dollar cushion for this effort to come to fruition—he is referring to sectors comparable to those we mentioned in the process of reequilibration. The parallel is with the disloyal opposition, which has left the democratic system, and the large number of passive supporters of democracy who are not ready to give it their support, who wait for an effort of the political class to solve the crisis, or remain unaware of, or unperturbed by, decline in quality. Those tolerant of the failures of democracy, unwilling to join the disloyal opposition, but not ready to demand total conformity with democratic principles, make the reequilibration process possible, even at the cost of democratic legality.

The question can be raised as to whether some of the nondemocratic regimes that were established through a combination of illegal, violent pressures and the formally legal investiture of the new government, particularly after a certain pacification of the country and some signs of efficacy, might not have developed into a new democratic regime in which the challengers would have become the hegemonic basis of a coalition. Perhaps Mussolini did not rule out such a possibility in 1922. The entry into the government of representatives of other parties, the vote of confidence he obtained, the benevolent neutrality of the General Confederation of Labor, which was ready to distance itself from the Socialist party, the attempt to curtail the violence of the squads, the initial successes in the economic field, and above all, the transformistic traditions of Italian politics, would have favored such a development. In this sense, it might seem that the Matteoti murder and its aftermath, which made Mussolini appear responsible for the violence of Fascist extremists and led to their pressure on him to protect them, caused him to opt for a fully authoritarian, if not totalitarian, alternative.

The concept of reequilibration in the Paretian tradition does not mean that the new equilibrium of forces within the constraints of the democratic process would be the same as before. Nor does it mean that within certain limits the rules of the game would not be modified, particularly the electoral laws, which can contribute so much to shaping the party system, or the relationships between executive and legislature. In fact, the changes required may reach the borderline between democracy and semiauthoritarian solutions if the new regime imposes certain limits on civil liberties or outlaws particular parties, as in the case of the Communist party in Finland in the 1930s. But might not a less democratic democracy, particularly if an opposition considered disloyal by large segments of the polity is outlawed, be a better alternative than risking civil war or an authoritarian regime in defense of democratic authenticity?

We have deliberately started our discussion of reequilibration with an emphasis on the most advanced stage in which change of regime occurs within the genus *democratic*, but patterns that are more likely, more viable, and less risky might be considered at an earlier stage of the breakdown process. In principle, all require parties committed to the democratic order to sacrifice their particular goals, the interests of many of their followers, and their ideological commitments, as well as accepting limits on the most libertarian interpretation of civil liberties, for the sake of stabilizing the situation and insuring survival of the system. In a sense they involve an oligopolistic solution that deviates from pure competition but avoids monopoly of power. Such solutions are characterized by national unity coalition governments, temporary postponements of elections, agreement between the parties not to compete in elections, and prearranged formulas to assure the parties rotation in office or proportional representation in key government posts. They reflect the actions of democracies in time of war, but the cases of Austria after World War II and Colombia after the Rojas Pinilla dictatorship are interesting examples of such efforts in post-crisis democracies. (For the latter, see the chapter by Alexander Wilde in part 3 of this project.)

These cases, as well as the proposals made for such solutions in crisis periods, would make interesting studies. In this context, the idea of a Spanish Republican dictatorship, advanced by democratic politicians uncommitted to either the Popular Front or the moderate Right in the spring of 1936, is particularly interesting. Could Azaña, aided by his considerable personal prestige, with the cooperation of CEDA moderates and the more moderate sectors of the Socialist party led by Prieto and supported by the bulk of the army, have succeeded in such a solution, thereby avoiding civil war or reducing it to local revolutions and pronunciamentos? Our qualified answer would be "probably." However, the cost of such extreme solutions might be too high for the participants, since they might involve a restructuring of the party system—a splitting of major parties and readiness to use considerable force. In fact, the greatest cost would be psychic, and the politicians faced with such a choice would be unlikely to take the risks involved. To betray lifetime commitments and loyalties is not easy, even for politicians, particularly when success is far from assured.

Our analysis of the extreme models of reequilibration has, among other purposes, aimed at highlighting the degrees of freedom open to the political leadership even in extreme situations. It is only the execution of such mental experiments, combined with the effort to understand (*verstehen*) the actors, that will advance our knowledge about processes of political change, even when that process might be an obstacle to the building of elegant causal models.[4]

Restoration and Reinstauration of Democracy

Founding a new democracy and consolidating it after a relatively short period of nondemocratic rule, with many leaders of the earlier democratic regime playing major roles, is not strictly a case of reequilibration.[5] It differs decisively from those cases in which the autocratic period has lasted many years and its persecution of democratic leaders has been so thorough that few have returned to political life. The passing of time implies that new generations who have no identification with the predictatorship parties and leadership will have entered political life. New leaders will then found a new regime that might see little reason to claim to be a legitimate continuation of the previous regime and thus to represent a case of instauration rather than restoration.[6] Most cases of the return to democracy might be somewhere in between.

The restoration situation poses some special problems, created by the need to overcome tension between the parties that contributed to the breakdown, to eliminate suspicion of past semiloyal actions, and to avoid reaffirmation of policies and ideological positions that contributed to the crisis. This will all be influenced by the extent to which the leadership of the reestablished regime has learned from past experience. Will it reaffirm the positions of the past, raise again the divisive issues of that time, and unearth past recriminations against opponents to blame them for the breakdown? In this respect, the instauration of a new regime by new men may have some advantages for the consolidation of democracy. On the other hand, those who lived through a fateful crisis are likely to better understand the types of action that lead to the downfall of democracy, have more experience in democratic political procedures, and make better parliamentarians. They may be able to contribute knowledge and greater pragmatism to the consolidation of the regime, thereby avoiding some of the difficulties that occur in the consolidation stage of new democratic regimes and that contributed to the crisis of the previous one.

The reestablishment process will vary depending on the nature of the regime established after the fall of democracy. Certainly, totalitarian rule, by persecuting almost all the democratic leaders, is likely to have created considerable solidarity among them. To have been together in jails and concentration camps can create a readiness to work together among even the most bitter opponents. Such a regime also poses less ambiguity about the identity of leaders and supporters—particularly the identity of members of the single mobilization party. The principled exclusion of the old political class, even if some of its members would have been ready to collaborate with a new regime, makes it easy to define those who shall be allowed to play an active role in the restoration of democracy. Perhaps this has been one of the advantages in the process of rebuilding the democracies in Germany, Austria, and even Italy after World War II. Restoration after an authoritarian regime that coopted politicians active in the preceding regime, that persecuted some opponents and tolerated others, poses more serious problems. This is particularly true when some of the emerging parties use the past record of political leaders and parties as an argument to disqualify them from participating in political life. The Communists in Eastern Europe after World War II, particularly in Czechoslovakia, were very adroit in using this tactic.

This is not the place to pursue this problem, which will be touched upon in other chapters. It is important, however, to see that it underlines a problem central to macropolitical sociological analysis: continuity and discontinuity in the political process.

The Right to Disobedience, and Rebellion and Partisanship in Defense of Democracy

Can it be that our analysis itself is shaped by the conflict we are analyzing? Are our theories embedded in a tradition of both scientific inquiry and political discourse not made explicit? Are the terms we use consciously or unconsciously biased in favor of the regime against its opponents? A recent essay by Terry Nardin, the literature on civil disobedience, and recent analyses of violence in America raise such questions, which could be safely ignored in an analysis of the breakdown of democracies based on the paradigmatic case of the Weimar Republic, but not in that of other cases.[7]

It is important to keep in mind that the rebellion against democratic regimes is ultimately a conflict about legitimacy formulas. The rebels claim that the democratic authorities have forfeited their right to rule and that they have become illegitimate even within their own system of values.[8] The Weberian analysis of legitimacy emphasizes that limits are built in in each type of regime and that the transformation of regimes beyond them is a source of their delegitimation and their ultimate breakdown.[9] De Tocqueville warned especially of the dangers of oppression by the majority in a democracy.[10] Violation of constitutional norms, abuse of power, disregard of civil liberties, and excessive violence by the authorities cannot be ignored as cause for the breakdown of democracies. Certainly those overthrowing a regime will claim such abuses, and it is this claim that convinces many moderate nonpartisan citizens to support, or at least accept, the overthrow of a regime. In our terms it could be said that the actors disloyal to a democratic regime are those accorded power by democratic procedures: the legally elected government is the source of danger to the continuity and normal functioning of democratic institutions.

In the cases in our purview, that argument may be dismissed as self-serving, in view of the unwillingness of those who have used it to attain power to reestablish free democratic political processes, despite their claim of having overthrown a particular democratic government to save democracy. It is also belied by the willingness of such groups to enter into coalition with political groups that were disloyal to a democratic regime even before it allegedly violated the democratic trust. It could be argued, therefore, that such arguments have validity only when the overthrow of a particular government, the temporary crisis of a democratic regime, leads to the reestablishment of democracy. But this is an easy way out of a serious question, because it is unlikely that this disruption by violent means, even in the defense of democracy, can lead to the establishment or reequilibration of a democratic regime, irrespective of the intentions of the actors. Therefore, the outcome does not prove that the arguments used at the time were hypocritical or the allegations false.

From this perspective, the breakdown of democracy is caused not by the actions of a disloyal opposition, but by rulers who, though they have acquired power by constitutional democratic means, exercise it in such a way that the normal methods open to a loyal opposition for exercising its critique—the use of the constitutional mechanism for control of the government, the exercise of democratic liberal freedoms and waiting for the next election to make the rulers accountable for their abuse of power—begin to seem inadequate to assure the continuity of a democratic regime. European political theorists have formulated this situation in terms of the conflict between legality and legitimacy—in this case, democratic legitimacy.

It differs from situations in which the opposition to a regime is based on other legitimacy formulas. These might include the defense of traditional authority in the counterrevolutionary attacks on democracy in the nineteenth century, the charisma of a leader, the historical mission of a revolutionary movement or a class represented by its most conscious members, though they are an electoral minority, or a conception of the national community expressed by plebiscite rather than through the representation of interests in the society. In those cases, two conceptions of legitimacy conflict, both claiming the allegiance of the people. In the last analysis, citizens must decide to which side they will grant the right to use force, in view of their ultimate values, placing those values higher than values sustaining a democratic regime, if they cannot be permanently assured within the framework of the regime. No democratic regime can guarantee any set of ultimate values forever, since democracy is based on the assumption that from time to time the majority of citizens might favor different values. In fact, in stable democracies the compromises acceptable to most citizens on such ultimate values tend to be protected against rapidly changing majorities by the requirement that only qualified majorities can change them and, in some extreme cases of conflict, by giving the veto right even to a minority. As Schumpeter emphasized, a condition for the success of democracy, in contrast to the classical theory of democracy, is that the effective range of political decision should not be extended too far, and that not every function of the state should be subject to a democratic political method.[11]

Another question is whether one of the causes of breakdown of democracy is the anti- or ademocratic behavior of formally democratic rulers. This would mean a situation different from that in the final crisis of the Weimar Republic or in Italian democracy in the early twenties, when disloyal opposition and the loss of efficacy and effectiveness combined to produce a transfer of power to what was to be a new regime. Certainly, disloyal oppositions will always claim that the democratic authorities have betrayed their own principles, will always be among the most vocal defenders of civil liberties for themselves while denying them to others, and will always claim, sometimes with good reason, to be the victims of discrimination, persecution, and even illegal acts by the authorities. No one should be surprised to learn, in reading the autobiographies of Nazi activists collected by Abel, that they felt like an oppressed minority suffering police actions and social pressures brought to bear at the workplace, by excommunication from the church, and by family and friends.[12] At the same time, let it be noted, they boasted of readiness to use violence against their opponents. In fact, most democratic governments, faced with a disloyal opposition using violence and with leaders who publicly justify its use against a regime they define as illegitimate, are likely to use measures that would be and should be unacceptable against a loyal opposition. They may enact legislation banning the carrying of arms, wearing of uniforms, and organization of paramilitary units, forbidding membership in such organizations by police or army officers and civil servants, and banning demonstrations whose clear purpose is to provoke violence.[13]

Such measures taken in defense of democracy, even when legally enacted by democratic majorities in the legislatures, can be and have been questioned from a strict civil libertarian point of view.[14] Their adoption undoubtedly involves the risk of what Continental legal theorists call *abus du droit*, that is, the use of legal norms for purposes for which they were not intended. It occurs when these stringent measures are extended to opponents who cannot be considered to constitute a violent disloyal opposition. At this point the defense of democracy might become delegitimizing for those who do not support the disloyal opposition. In this twilight zone it begins to be difficult to distinguish between those who question the authority on grounds legitimate within the democratic framework and those who are semiloyal because, while disapproving of the methods of the disloyal opposition, they agree with its ultimate goals. Indeed, they might even consider a coalition with it in view of their own aims or some shared goals. Then the struggle begins for the minds of those without strong commitment to the existing political or social order and those committed to its overthrow.

That struggle is well described by Pareto in this classic text:

Theories designed to justify the use of force by the governed are almost always combined with theories condemning the use of force by the public authority. A few dreamers reject the use of force in general, on whatever side; but their theories either have no influence at all or else serve merely to weaken resistance on the part of people in power, so clearing the field for violence on the part of the governed. In view of that we may confine ourselves to considering such theories, in general, in the combined form.

No great number of theories are required to rouse to resistance and to the use of force people who are, or think they are, oppressed. The derivations therefore are chiefly designed to incline people who would otherwise be neutral in the struggle to condemn resistance on the part of the governing powers, and so to make their resistance less vigorous; or at a venture, to persuade the rulers themselves in that sense.[15]

In a democratic regime and in a society where many people have accepted democratic legitimacy, the most telling argument in that ideological battle will be an effort to distinguish formal democratic legitimacy reduced to legality from genuine democracy, which may be defined as the responsiveness of the rulers to the real will of the people. That will cannot be manifested through formal democracy. Radical critics, including the Fascists, have argued that civil liberties are insufficient, given the inequalities in resources of different groups in the society, particularly in view of the control of economic means necessary for political action. Partisans of this position use as evidence the private ownership of mass media or their control by the government, the informal sanctions of the society against radical supporters at the workplace, for example, the commitment of all established institutions to the existing social and political order, the essentially conservative bias of the whole culture, and most recently, the pervasive influence of the consumption-oriented society that promotes individual aspirations rather than collective action, and material goals rather than the transformation of power relations.[16] The radicals undoubtedly have a point. But who can say whether their failure to mobilize democratically those whom they claim to represent is a result of those constraints or of the lack of attractiveness of their program and leadership?

There are enormous differences between societies in this respect. We would be the last to argue that the introduction of liberal democratic institutions and political processes in underdeveloped countries, or in traditional societies where the cultural and social relations support an existing social order, could lead to a rapid and peaceful transformation through the political mobilization of the underprivileged. It is tempting to substitute the decisive action of minorities, confident in their interpretation of the "real" needs of the people, for the slow process of mobilization through political parties and mass organizations. Barred from access to power through electoral means and the influence on public opinion, a self-conscious elite, claiming to speak for the silent masses, is likely to reject political democracy in the name of its identification with inarticulate majorities. In the ideological arsenal, the concept of false consciousness offers such a minority an easy way out. The inevitable consequence is the rejection of political democracy and the advocacy of dictatorship by the conscious minority—presumably dictatorship aiming to create the preconditions for *real* democracy: that is, one giving the people a real opportunity to participate. It was in this sense that Marx understood the dictatorship of the proletariat as the emergency organization of the revolutionary act, as an instrument to destroy the state, which was as the tool of the ruling class, as an instrument that would itself wither away. Sartori has rightly noted that in Marx's own time, the term, which he incidentally uses only in three places, did not have the derogatory meaning attached to it today.[17] It was Lenin who changed the emphasis and argued that the dictatorship of the proletariat is more democratic than bourgeois democracy, in this classic text:

The dictatorship of the proletariat, i.e., the organization of the vanguard of the oppressed as the ruling class for the purpose of suppressing the oppressors, cannot result merely in an expansion of democracy. *Simultaneously* with an immense expansion of democracy, *which for the first time* becomes a democracy for the poor, democracy for the people, and not democracy for the money bags, the dictatorship of the proletariat imposes a series of restrictions on the freedom of the oppressors, the exploiters, the capitalists. We must suppress them . . . their resistance must be crushed by force; and it is clear that where there is suppression, where there is violence, there is no freedom and no democracy.[18]

The point is not to discuss Leninist theory and the relationship between democracy and the Communist society, but to recognize that Lenin's analysis argues that the Marxist-Leninist is always automatically democratic, whereas all others are always automatically nondemocratic. We do not have to turn to anti-Marxist critics to appreciate the dangerous implications of his thought; Rosa Luxemburg did it brilliantly in her analysis of the Russian revolution when she wrote:

Yes, dictatorship! But this dictatorship consists in the *manner of applying democracy,* not in its *elimination,* in energetic, resolute attacks upon the well-entrenched rights and economic relationships of bourgeois society, without which a socialist transformation cannot be accomplished. But this dictatorship must be the work of the *class* and not of a little leading minority in the name of the class—that is, it must proceed step by step out of the active participation of the masses; it must be under their direct influence, subjected to the control of complete public activity; it must arise out of the growing political training of the mass of the people.[19]

And she continues her eloquent testimony:

Freedom only for the supporters of the government, only for the members of one party—however numerous they may be—is no freedom at all. Freedom is always and exclusively freedom for the one who thinks differently. Not because of any fanatical concept of "justice" but because all that is instructive, wholesome and purifying in political freedom depends on this essential characteristic, and its effectiveness vanishes when "freedom" becomes a special privilege.[20]

Let us be clear, therefore, that political democracy does not necessarily assure even a reasonable approximation of what we would call a democratic society, a society with considerable equality of opportunity in all spheres, including *social* equality, as well as opportunity to formulate political alternatives and mobilize the electorate for them. We should also be clear that dictatorships by a minority, a party self-appointed as spokesmen for a class, or the "people" assumed to be the majority, has never led to a regime that would satisfy a formulation like Rosa Luxemburg's.

There is, however, considerable evidence that slowly, over time, political democracy as we have defined it has led to considerable progress in the direction of a democratic society. It has not reached it, but it has approached it in a few cases.

There can be little argument with those who reject political democracy, in view of its slow progress toward a democratic society.[21] They should be free to consider the problems we have discussed and the analyses in this book basically irrelevant. From their perspective, it probably makes little difference if some of the countries studied were ruled by a democracy inching toward a democratic society or by an authoritarian regime.[22] In fact, some of the goals they consider worth pursuing might be achieved as well or better by authoritarian regimes than by oligarchic or stalemated democracies. Authoritarian regimes, however, have other costs that we might not be ready to pay, and in our view they leave the problem of building legitimate and stable political institutions in the twentieth century unsolved. From this perspective, which we would not argue to be value-free, the problem of the breakdown of even imperfect political democracies seems relevant. The danger lies in indifference to the crises of democracies and in willingness to contribute to their acceleration, in the hope that crisis will lead to a revolutionary breakthrough toward a democratic society rather than mere political democracy. The vain hope of making democracies more democratic by undemocratic means has all too often contributed to regime crises and ultimately paved the way to autocratic rule.

Notes

1. For a good review of the literature, see John D. May, *Of the Conditions and Measures of Democracy* (Morristown, N.J.: General Learning Press, 1973). The discussion was initiated by a seminal article by Seymour M. Lipset, "Some Social Requisites of Democracy: Economic Development and Political Legitimacy," *American Political Science Review* 53 (1959):69–105. Other major contributions to the debate were Harry Eckstein, "A Theory of Stable Democracy," appended to his *Division and Cohesion in Democracy: A Study of Norway* (Princeton, N.J.: Princeton University Press, 1966); and Robert A. Dahl, *Polyarchy: Participation and Opposition* (New Haven: Yale University Press, 1971). For a critical analysis, see Brian M. Barry, *Sociologists, Economists, and Democracy* (London: Collier-Macmillan, 1970), chap. 3. See also the collection of papers in the reader edited by Charles F. Cnudde and Deane E. Neubauer, *Empirical Democratic Theory* (Chicago: Markham, 1969).

2. In addition to the already quoted efforts of Lipset and Dahl, we can mention those of Phillips Cutright, "National Political Development: Its Measurement and Social Correlates," in *Politics and Social Life*, ed. Nelson W. Polsby, Robert A. Dentler, and Paul A. Smith (New York: Houghton Mifflin, 1963); and Deane E. Neubauer, "Some Conditions of Democracy," *American Political Science Review* 61 (December 1967):1002–9. On the much broader problem of the stability of political systems, democratic or not, the essay by Ted Robert Gurr, "Persistence and Change in Political Systems, 1800–1971," *American Political Science Review* 68 (December 1974):1482–1504, deserves special notice. See also Leon Hurwitz, "Democratic Political Stability: Some Traditional Hypotheses Reexamined," *Comparative Political Studies* 4 (January 1972):476–90; and idem, "An Index of Democratic Political Stability: A New Methodological Note," *Comparative Political Studies* 4 (April 1971):41–68.

3. In this respect the work of the historian-political scientist Karl Dietrich Bracher, beginning with his theoretical-historical essay "Auflösung einer Demokratie: Des Ende der Weimarer Republik als Forschungsproblem," in *Faktoren der Machtbildung*, ed. Arkadij Gurland (Berlin: Duncker and Humblot, 1952), pp. 39–98, has been pathbreaking. Our analysis has been inspired by and owes much to his thinking and monumental work.

4. Let us warn the reader that he will not find in this essay or in the chapters in this volume any formal model susceptible to computer simulation. Neither our training, the state of our knowledge, nor the complexity of the problem warranted it, but we would certainly welcome other scholars to try such a formulation of our efforts. For an example of how less formal analyses can be translated into a quite different language and scientific style, see Roland F. Moy, *A Computer Simulation of Democratic Political Development: Tests of the Lipset and Moore Models,* Comparative Politics Series, no. 01–019, vol. 2 (Beverly Hills, Ca.: Sage Professional Papers, 1971).

5. It would be interesting to study comparatively and systematically to what extent different participants, particularly the democratic leaders, were or were not aware of the dangers to the system at critical junctures before the final breakdown. For example, the statement of SPD (German Social-Democratic party) leader Breitscheid at the party congress in Magdeburg in 1929 about the implications of a breakup of the great coalition (which took place in March 1930) reveals both awareness of the threat to democracy and parliamentarianism and

unwillingness to make any sacrifice to save them. See Werner Conze, "Die Krise des Parteienstaates in Deutschland, 1929–30," in Gotthard Jasper, *Von Weimar zu Hitler, 1930–1933* (Cologne: Kiepenheuer and Witsch, 1968), p. 44. Even more foreboding were the pleas of Indalecio Prieto, the Spanish Socialist leader, in the spring of 1936, quoted in my chapter on Spain.

6. See the chapters on Latin American cases.

7. Our basic starting point is Max Weber's formulation, "methodological individualism." It is well stated in a 1920 letter quoted by Wolfgang J. Mommsen, "Diskussion über 'Max Weber und die Machtpolitik,'" in *Verhandungen des 15 deutschen Soziologentages: Max Weber und die Soziologie heute* (Tübingen: J. C. B. Mohr [Paul Siebeck], 1965), p. 137, as follows: "Sociology can be pursued only by starting from the actions of the one, few or many individuals [einzelnen]; strictly individualistic in the method. . . . The State in its sociological meaning is nothing but the probability [chance] that certain forms of specific actions shall take place. Actions of specific individual human beings. Nothing else. . . . the subjective in it that the actions are oriented by specific conceptions. The objective is that we the observers feel that there is a probability that these actions oriented by those conceptions will take place. If there is no such probability the State does not exist any more."

8. Our view of the social and political process conceives of historical situations as " . . . a relatively delicate balance between the forces working in radically opposed directions, so that the difference made by a war, a political movement, or even the influence of a single man may be of very far-reaching consequences . . . . It is not that such a factor 'creates' the result. It is rather that, in addition to the other forces working in that direction, it is sufficient to throw the total balance in favor of the one possible outcome rather than the other." Max Weber, in Reinhard Bendix, *Max Weber: An Intellectual Portrait* (London: Heinemann, 1960), p. 269. Incidentally, Sir James Jeans uses the same image: "The course of a railway train is uniquely prescribed for it at most points of its journey by the rails on which it runs. Here and there, however, it comes to a junction at which alternative courses are open to it, and it may be turned on to one or the other by the quite negligible expenditure of energy involved in moving the points." Quoted by Albert Speer in *Inside the Third Reich* (New York: Avon, 1971), p. 55.

9. Bracher, "Anflösung einer Demokratie."

10. For a stimulating discussion of the role of precipitating causes, see Robert McIver, *Social Causation* (Boston: Ginn and Co., 1942), esp. chap. 6, pp. 161–94.

11. Leadership is, for our purposes, a residual variable that ultimately—as the preceding text by Weber noted—cannot be ignored; but it should not be introduced before the explanatory power of other variables has been exhausted. In some cases, however, its contribution is so obvious that it should be given its due: For example, in our discussion of the reequilibration of French democracy in the transition from the Fourth to the Fifth Republic. The outcome there without de Gaulle would probably have been quite different. The problem of leadership and its quality—particularly in crisis situations—as an independent variable has tended to be neglected due to an overreaction against "great men in history" approaches and an overemphasis on sociological factors. See Lewis Edinger, "The Comparative Analysis of Political Leadership." For recent studies, see Lewis J. Edinger, ed., *Political Leadership: Studies in Comparative Analysis* (New York: John Wiley and Sons, 1967), and the Summer 1968 issue of *Daedalus*, entitled "Philosophers and Kings: Studies in Leadership."

12. The expression was coined by Ignazio Silone and serves as title to his book *The School for Dictators* (London: Jonathan Cape, 1939), a witty and insightful work that is very relevant for the readers of this volume. (Perhaps someone should write a "School for Democrats.")

13. On the problem of defining political democracy in terms that are both meaningful and operational, see Giovanni Sartori, *Democratic Theory* (Detroit, Mich.: Wayne State University Press, 1962); Dahl, *Polyarchy;* and the classic statements by Hans Kelsen, *Vom Wesen und Wert der Demokratie* (Tübingen: J. C. B. Mohr, 1929), and "Foundations of Democracy," *Ethics* 66 (October 1955), pt. 2.

14. See Juan J. Linz, "Totalitarian and Authoritarian Regimes," in *Handbook of Political Science,* ed. Fred I. Greenstein and Nelson W. Polsby (Reading, Mass.: Addison-Wesley, 1975), vol. 3, pp. 175–411, for a characterization of those different types of regimes and some considerations about the dynamics of change in and of them. The problem of decay, breakdown, and its aftermath in Iberian authoritarian regimes is discussed in Juan J. Linz,

"Spain and Portugal: Critical Choices," in *Western Europe: The Trials of Partnership*, ed. David S. Landes (Lexington, Mass: D. C. Heath, 1977), pp. 237–96.

15. The question of freedom for antidemocratic parties, particularly those advocating the use of force to overthrow democratic regimes, is a complex one. The question of legal repression of political organizations while upholding liberal institutions is discussed in Otto Kirchheimer, *Political Justice: The Use of Legal Procedures for Political Ends* (Princeton, N.J.: Princeton University Press, 1961), chap. 4, pp. 132–72, with particular emphasis on the West German application of constitutional provisions to the KPD and the right-wing SRP. For an analysis of the situation in the thirties, see Karl Loewenstein, "Legislative Control of Political Extremism in European Democracies," *Columbia Law Review* 38, no. 4 (April 1938), and no. 5 (May 1938), pp. 725–74.

16. The idea that at least one successful alternation in power at the national level between the democratic regime-instauring party or coalition and the opposition would be required to define a regime as democratic seems to us too stringent. Certainly, alternation of government and opposition at the national level is not frequent, even in two-party democracies. See Giovanni Sartori, "Il caso italiano: Salvare il pluralismo e superare la polarizzazione," *Revista Italiana di Sciènza Polìtica* 3 (1974):675–87 and 676–78. It is even less likely in multiparty systems, where shifting coalitions are frequent occurrences.

17. See Linz, "Totalitarian and Authoritarian Regimes," pp. 336–50. To get a sense of the limited change that the Dubček reforms represented in principle, see Alex Pravda, "Reform and Change in the Czechoslovak Political System: January–August 1968," Sage Research Papers in the Social Sciences (Beverly Hills, Ca.: Sage, 1975).

18. See the chapters on Venezuela and Colombia in this volume. The extensive literature on Austrian politics after World War II makes constant reference to this "learning."

19. Victor S. Mamatey and Radomir Luza, eds., *A History of the Czechoslovak Republic, 1918–1948* (Princeton, N.J.: Princeton University Press, 1973).

20. There is by now an extensive literature on this type of democracy. See, for example, Arend Lijphart, *Democracy in Plural Societies: A Comparative Exploration* (New Haven, Yale University Press, 1977). For a bibliography and selection of texts, see Kenneth D. McRae, ed., *Consociational Democracy: Political Accommodation in Segmented Societies* (Toronto: McClelland and Stewart, 1974). The concept, however, has not remained unchallenged. See Brian Barry, "Review Article: Political Accommodation and Consociational Democracy," *British Journal of Political Science* 5, no. 4 (1975):477–505.

21. The Weimar Republic lasted only from 1918 to 1933, if we include the period before the approval of the constitution and the presidential rather than parliamentary governments of the early thirties. However, it would be a mistake to ignore the largely liberal and incipiently democratic period under the Empire, in which the parties organized and free elections, both to the Reichstag and Länder legislatures, took place regularly. Even the Spanish Republic, proclaimed on 14 April 1931 and doomed on 18 July 1936, came after a century in which liberalism and democracy had imposed itself—with more or less success—and after forty-seven years of peaceful constitutional (or at least semiconstitutional) monarchy (1876–1923). The Italian liberal and increasingly (with the expansion of suffrage) democratic state had even deeper roots in the Risorgimento and unification periods.

22. The problem of durability has been analyzed in Harry Eckstein, *The Evaluation of Political Performance: Problems and Dimensions* (Beverly Hills, Ca.: Sage, 1971), pp. 21–32, and in Ted Robert Gurr and Muriel McClelland, *Political Performance: A Twelve-Nation Study* (Beverly Hills, Ca.: Sage, 1971), pp. 10–17.

23. Robert A. Dahl and Edward R. Tufte, in *Size and Democracy* (Stanford, Ca.: Stanford University Press, 1973), analyze thoroughly the hypotheses advanced on the ways in which small size might contribute to democracy.

24. See Klaus Epstein's review of books by Joseph Berlau, Peter Gay, and Carl Schorske in *World Politics* 11 (1959):629–51, and the concluding chapter in Guenther Roth, *The Social Democrats in Imperial Germany: A Study in Working-Class Isolation and National Integration* (Totowa, N.J.: Bedminster Press, 1963).

25. In this context, the book by Barrington Moore, *Social Origins of Dictatorship and Democracy* (Boston: Beacon Press, 1966), deserves mention. His deliberate neglect of the smaller states is compensated for in the following works: Dahl, *Polyarchy*; Hans Daalder, "Building Consociational Nations," in *Building States and Nations*, ed. S. N. Eisenstadt and Stein

Rokkan (Beverly Hills, Ca.: Sage, 1973), vol. 2, *Analyses by Region*, pp. 15–31; Dankwart Rustow, "Sweden's Transition to Democracy: Some Notes toward a Genetic Theory," *Scandinavian Political Studies* 6 (1971): 9–26; and Francis G. Castles, "Barrington Moore's Thesis and Swedish Political Development," *Government and Opposition* 8, no. 3 (1973): 313–31.

26. Austria in the twenties saw periods in which the main "camps" were able to overcome their differences; the Baltic republics, after gaining their independence and enduring short civil wars followed by thorough agrarian reforms, seemed destined for stability; and even the Weimar Republic at one point seemed on the way to stabilization. On the other hand, we have countries like Belgium, which have experienced serious political crises without experiencing any serious danger to their democratic institutions. Our analysis, therefore, should be complemented by the study of periods of consolidation and stabilization of democracy, and of successful weathering of crises.

27. Richard Rose, "Dynamic Tendencies in the Authority of Regimes," *World Politics* 21, no. 4 (July 1969):602–28.

28. Friedrich Meinecke, *The German Catastrophe: Reflections and Recollections* (Cambridge, Mass.: Harvard University Press, 1950), p. 63. He writes: "I said to myself with the deepest consternation not only that a day of misfortune of the first order had dawned for Germany, but also, 'This was not necessary.' Here existed no pressing political or historical necessity such as had led to the downfall of William II in the Autumn of 1918. Here it was no general tendency, but something like chance, specifically Hindenburg's weakness, that had turned the scales."

29. In his classic typology of authority, Weber does not explicitly discuss the distinction between democratic (or "polyarchic," to use Dahl's terminology) and nondemocratic regimes, but there is an obvious overlap between his type of legal-rational authority and democratic regimes as we have defined them. As he deliberately avoided the problems posed by the natural law critics—emphasizing considerations of substantive justice rather than "formal" justice—we have avoided the question of responsiveness in democracies in favor of a criterion of formal accountability that has the advantage of relatively easy empirical verification. On this distinction, see Juan J. Linz, "Michels e il suo contributo alla sociologia politica." Introduction to Roberto Michels, *La sociologia del partito politico nella democrazia moderna* (Bologna: Il Mulino, 1966), pp. lxxxi–xcii.

30. The natural law tradition inevitably places justice above formal legality and "general principles of law" above enacted laws, but offers no unequivocal means of ascertaining what they are, unless we would turn to the claims made by the Catholic church to define what is "natural," *sive recta rationis*. Such a claim has been used by Catholic thinkers to justify tyrannicide and the right to rebellion, and in the American Protestant and secular tradition of "civil disobedience." For Catholic thought, see Heinrich A. Rommen, *The State in Catholic Thought: A Treatise in Political Philosophy* (St. Louis, Mo.: Herder, 1945), pp. 473–76. Both can also serve minorities who want to challenge, even violently, the actions of legally elected authorities acting constitutionally when these authorities are perceived as threatening ultimate values. This was the argument used by some Catholics to justify the uprising against the Republican government in Spain; see the influential book by Aniceto de Castro Albarrán, *El derecho a la rebeldía* (Madrid: Imp. Gráfica Universal, 1934).

31. The distinction between a denial of legitimacy to the political system and its denial to the socioeconomic system is basically analytical. In reality the two are difficult to distinguish. Certainly a deep hatred toward a socioeconomic order almost inevitably leads to denial of legitimacy to the political system should the system sustain that social order or even allow its reestablishment. Since a democracy (as we have defined it) assures the survival of such a hated order if the majority supports it, or allows the temporarily defeated minority to argue freely for its restoration, the rejection of democracy in that case would be a logical consequence. Similarly, those who value a socioeconomic order so highly that the prospect of even a temporary democratically imposed change would be unacceptable will turn against democracy. A more serious question arises if we argue that free competition in regular elections for the power to implement alternative programs requires organizational and economic resources, and a degree of personal independence, which can only be guaranteed by a free disposal of resources by groups and individuals escaping the control of the government

and its supporters. More concretely, if the socialization of property and income beyond basic individual needs, and the integration into single-interest organizations privileged by and dependent on the government, would deprive the opposition of any opportunity to organize its appeal, we would conclude that the establishment of such a socioeconomic and institutional order is incompatible with political democracy. Paradoxically, the liberals fearful of socialism and those who argue that in a classless Socialist society there is no need for competition between parties agree in their ultimate conclusion.

32. Meinecke, *German Catastrophe,* pp. 63–65, rightly stresses the importance of this point in the interpretation of the historical process. It is also decisive in determining whether the defense of democracy is possible, since the alternative view, which links the outcome of the conflict inevitably with underlying structural problems, external factors, cultural traditions, etc., undermines the defenders' faith in their success, and therefore their will. It also contributes to the willingness of others to pursue their goals "preventively," without waiting for change within a democratic framework that is ultimately doomed.

33. The ideological ambiguity of maximalist Marxist socialism in contrast to social-democratic reformism—first formulated by Bernstein—has often been noted but not systematically studied. A good analysis of one of its variants is Norbert Leser, *Zwischen Reformismus und Bolschewismus: Der Austromarxismus als Theorie und Praxis* (Vienna: Europa, 1968). Another is Erich Matthias, "Kautsky und der Kautskyanismus: Die Funktion der Ideologie in der deutschen Sozialdemokratie vor dem ersten Weltkrieg," in *Marxismusstudien,* ed. Iring Fetscher, (Tübingen: J. C. B. Mohr, 1957), vol. 2., pp. 151–97. Even in Harold Laski's *Democracy in Crisis* (Chapel Hill, N. C.: University of North Carolina Press, 1933), we find this ambiguous formulation applied to the United Kingdom in the thirties: "I believe, therefore, that the attainment of power by the Labour Party in the normal electoral fashion must result in a radical transformation of parliamentary government. Such an administration could not, if it sought to be effective, accept the present forms of its procedure. It would have to take vast powers, and legislate under them by ordinance and decree; it would have to suspend the classic formulae of normal opposition. If its policy met with peaceful acceptance, the continuance of parliamentary government would depend upon its possession of guarantees from the Conservative Party that its work of transformation would not be disrupted by repeal in the event of its defeat at the polls."

34. Obviously there will be those who sincerely feel that other human values rank higher, and who, if democracy cannot insure those values because an "unenlightened" electorate lacks the proper "consciousness of its interests," will be prepared to bend democracy and the civil liberties it presupposes to their wishes or threaten revolutionary action should it be an obstacle to them. Certainly in the face of poverty, inequality, economic stagnation, and national dependency on foreign powers accepted by democratic rulers (for example, the Weimar politicians accepting with reservations an *Erfüllungspolitik*), such a response is understandable. However, those who think this way should be very sure that the odds in a nonelectoral struggle are in their favor; they should remember that for each successful revolution there have been more victorious counterrevolutions that have represented not only the maintenance of the status quo but often a loss of gains already made and terrible costs for those advocating such radical changes.

CHAPTER 2

1. This point is well developed in M. Rainer Lepsius, "Machtübernähme und Machtübergäbe: Zur Strategie des Regimewechsels," in *Sozialtheorie und Soziale Praxis: Homage to Eduard Baumgarten,* Mannheimer Sozialwissenschaftliche Studien, vol. 3, ed. Hans Albert et al. (Meisenheim: Anton Hain, 1971), pp. 158–73.

2. Popular revolutions (*strictu sensu*), particularly Marxist-inspired revolutions, have not succeeded in countries with liberal and relatively democratic institutions. The attempts made in Germany and Finland at the end of World War I and the October revolution in Asturias

(Spain) failed; the revolutionary climate in northern Italy in 1919 came to nothing. Even some of the attempts in more autocratic countries, such as Hungary, have also failed. The successful revolutions of the twentieth century have been against nondemocratic regimes: Mexico, Russia, Yugoslavia, China, and Cuba, and in colonial countries in the process of gaining independence, such as Vietnam and Algeria. In the case of Russia, China, and Yugoslavia, war was a major contributing factor. Nine of the peasant-based revolutions in Mexico, Russia, China, Vietnam, Algeria, and Cuba studied by Eric Wolf in *Peasant Wars of the Twentieth Century* (New York: Harper and Row, 1969) were directed against minimally established democratic regimes. As Edward Malefakis has noted, the Spanish peasantry in the revolutionary civil war was divided between the two sides and did not constitute the core of the revolutionary forces. In addition, its revolutionary mobilization during the Republic was limited, and it had no role in the October revolution. See "Peasants, Politics, and Civil War in Spain, 1931-1936," in *Modern European Social History*, ed. Robert Bezucha (Lexington, Mass.: D. C. Heath, 1972), pp. 192-227.

3. Whether or not to consider the Nazi impact on German society revolutionary depends on one's concept of revolution. Obviously, if only changes in the ownership of the means of production define revolution, Hitler's rule was not revolutionary. If we consider radical changes in the status structure, the position of the army and the churches, control of the economy, and above all, the values of the society as being the defining factors, it certainly was a revolution. Even if we consider changes toward equality as the defining factor, the leveling of traditional German status distinctions by inverting the social hierarchies in and by the party, even the equality before despotic arbitrary power, we could argue that it was revolutionary.

    The changes in German society that were planned and, in part, realized, which are described by David Schoenbaum in *Hitler's Social Revolution: Class and Status in Nazi Germany, 1933-1939* (Garden City, N.Y.: Doubleday, 1963), are different from those resulting from most breakdowns of democracy in Europe. See also Ralf Dahrendorf, *Society and Democracy in Germany* (Garden City, N.Y.: Doubleday, 1969), pp. 381-96, for an insightful discussion of the "unintended" modernizing effect of the National Socialist revolution on German society.

4. In this context see Eckstein, *Evaluation of Political Performance*, pp. 32-50. Even where political violence contributes ultimately to the breakdown of a regime, the peak of the violence does not necessarily coincide with the final phase. Civil war, putsches, and assassinations characterized the early years of the Weimar Republic and were followed by a phase of consolidation, but they left a legacy of disloyalty and skepticism about the regime. In Spain, the revolution of October 1934 did not produce a breakdown but wounded the system deeply. For an example of the time series needed to relate both phenomena and the different components of violence, see "Political Protest and Executive Change," Section 3 of Charles L. Taylor and Michael C. Hudson, *World Handbook of Political and Social Indicators* (New Haven: Yale University Press, 1972), pp. 59-199. One of the more sophisticated comparative analyses is Ivo K. Feierabend, with Rosalind L. Feierabend and Betty A. Nesvold, "The Comparative Study of Revolution and Violence," *Comparative Politics* 5, no. 3 (April 1973):393-424 (with bibliographic references). It was initiated by the earlier work of Ted Robert Gurr, including (with Charles Ruttenberg) *The Conditions of Civil Violence: First Tests of a Causal Model*, Princeton University, Center of International Studies, Research Monograph no. 28 (Princeton, N.J., 1967). See also Douglas A. Hibbs, Jr., *Mass Political Violence: A Cross-National Causal Analysis* (New York: Wiley, 1973). Unfortunately, there are no comparable cross-national studies of internal violence in the interwar years to contrast the rates of violence in countries experiencing a breakdown of regimes, those not experiencing a breakdown, and contemporary rates. Nor is it easy, as we shall note, to relate the different measures of violence—rate, intensity, type, location—with the problem of stability of regimes. Certainly, northern Italian violence was high before 1922, but the south was relatively quiescent; the pervasive threat of violence caused by the Nazi SA presence is difficult to compare with the more deadly actions of the *squadristi*, etc. This would be an interesting area for comparative historical research.

5. An excellent example is Peter Merkl, *Political Violence under the Swastika: 581 Early Nazis* (Princeton, N.J.: Princeton University Press, 1975). There is no comparable study of Italian

squadrismo. The reaction of the authorities and the courts toward political violence also deserves study. For Weimar Germany we have the work of Emil J. Gumbel, *Vom Fememord zur Reichskanzlei* (Heidelberg: Lambert Schneider, 1962), based on his studies in the twenties, like *Zwei Jahre Mord* (Berlin: Neues Vaterland, 1921), but there are no comparable analyses of judicial treatment of violence in Italy, Austria, or Spain in the crisis period.

6. The ambiguities in the German case are well discussed in Hans Schneider, "Das Ermächtigungsgesetz vom 24, März 1933," in *Von Weimar zu Hitler: 1930-1933*, ed. Gotthard Jasper (Cologne: Kiepenheuer and Witsch, 1968) pp. 405-42, which quotes the relevant literature. See also Hans Boldt, "Article 48 of the Weimar Constitution: Its Historical and Political Implications," in *German Democracy and the Triumph of Hitler*, ed. Anthony Nicholls and Erich Matthias (London: Georg Allen and Unwin, 1971), pp. 79-98. This is one of the few cases in which legality came into conflict with democratic legitimacy, one in which legal procedures were used to achieve ends in clear conflict with the basic assumptions of democratic legitimacy. The bureaucracies and the armed forces—particularly in the German/Prussian tradition—were more bound to legality, positivistically understood, than committed to liberal-democratic values, which facilitated the Nazi *Machtergreifung* and consolidation in power enormously. It assured the new rulers the loyalty of many who would be far from being their supporters.

7. We regret that we have not included an analysis of the breakdown or overthrow of democracy in Czechoslovakia in 1948. Obviously the pressures and the more or less direct intervention of the Soviet Union make this a special case. See Josef Korbel, *Communist Subversion of Czechoslovakia, 1938-1948: The Failure of Co-existence* (Princeton, N.J.: Princeton University Press, 1959) and Pavel Tigrid, "The Prague Coup of 1948: The Elegant Takeover," in *The Anatomy of Communist Takeovers*, ed. Thomas T. Hammond and Robert Farrell (New Haven: Yale University Press, 1975), with bibliographic references to Western and recent Czech sources. The same can be said for the sequence of events leading to the secession of Slovakia after the Munich *diktat* and the internal transformation of the Czech remainder state before its incorporation into Germany as the *Reichsprotektorat*.

8. Max Weber, in *Economy and Society*, ed. Guenther Roth and Claus Wittich (New York: Bedminster Press, 1968), pp. 212-13 stated:

> Domination was defined above (ch. I:16) as the probability that certain specific commands (or all commands) will be obeyed by a given group of persons. It thus does not include every mode of exercising "power" or "influence" over other persons. Domination ("authority") in this sense may be based on the most diverse motives of compliance: all the way from simple habituation to the most purely rational calculation of advantage. Hence every genuine form of domination implies a minimum of voluntary compliance, that is, an *interest* (based on ulterior motives or genuine acceptance) in obedience. Normally the rule over a considerable number of persons requires a staff (cf. ch. I:12), that is, a *special* group which can normally be trusted to execute the general policy as well as the specific commands. The members of the administrative staff may be bound to obedience to their superior (or superiors) by custom, by affectual ties, by a purely material complex of interests, or by ideal (*wertrationale*) motives. The quality of these motives largely determines the type of domination. *Purely* material interests and calculations of advantages as the basis of solidarity between the chief and his administrative staff result, in this as in other connexions, in a relatively unstable situation. Normally, other elements, affectual and ideal, supplement such interests. In certain exceptional cases the former alone may be decisive. In everyday life these relationships, like others, are governed by custom and material calculation of advantage.

9. Ibid., p. 213.

10. John F. Kennedy, during the Oxford, Mississippi, crisis, as quoted in the *New York Times*, 1 October 1962, p. 22.

11. Ibid.

12. "Multiple sovereignty is the identifying feature of revolutions. A revolution begins when a government previously under the control of a single, sovereign polity becomes the object of effective, competing, mutually exclusive claims on the part of two or more distinct polities; it ends when a single sovereign polity regains control over government." Charles Tilly,

"Revolutions and Collective Violence," in Greenstein and Polsby, *Handbook of Political Science*, vol. 3, p. 519. This excellent essay coincides in many points with our analysis and complements it in other respects. Tilly's critical review of other approaches saves us from the need to do such a review here.

13. This is not the place to quote the extensive bibliography on military interventions in politics. See Linz, "Totalitarian and Authoritarian Regimes," for a brief review of the problem and references to the literature. A recent addition to the growing literature on the subject is William R. Thompson, "Regime Vulnerability and the Military Coup," *Comparative Politics* 7, no. 4 (1975):459–87, which has extensive bibliographic references. Alfred Stepan, in *The Military in Politics: Changing Patterns in Brazil* (Princeton, N.J.: Princeton University Press, 1974), and in his chapter in this volume, shows how military intervention must be seen in the light of the actions of democratic rulers along the lines suggested in this essay, and not just from a perspective centered almost exclusively on the military.

14. On this point, see Juan J. Linz, "The Bases of Political Diversity in West German Politics" (Ph.D. diss., Columbia University, 1959). See also the chapter entitled "Cleavage and Consensus in West German Politics: The Early Fifties," in *Party Systems and Voter Alignments: Cross-National Perspectives*, ed. Seymour M. Lipset and Stein Rokkan, (New York: Free Press, 1967), pp. 305–16.

A fascinating set of data deserving further, sophisticated analysis is the long time series with identical or largely comparable questions on the overall support for prime ministers in different social groups and across party lines. Such diffuse support, tolerance, or rejection is one component and indicator of the willingness to grant legitimacy to a regime. See, for example: Pierpaolo Luzzato Fegiz, *Il volto sconosciuto dell' Italia: Dièci anni di sondagi Doxa* (Milan: Giuffrè, 1956), pp. 534–47; idem, *Il volto sconosciuto dell' Italia: Seconda serie, 1956–1965* (Milan: Giuffrè, 1966), pp. 865–99; and Elisabeth Noelle and Erich Peter Neumann, ed., *Jahrbuch der Öffentlichen Meinung*, 1965–1967, Allensbach, Institut für Demoskopie, 1967, Ib. *Jahrbuch der Öffentlichen Meinung 1968 bis 1973*, ib. 1974.

15. This point has been made with incomparable irony by Vilfredo Pareto in *The Mind and Society: A Treatise on General Sociology*, 2 vols. (New York: Dover, 1965), no. 585.

16. The mixed character of the bases of legitimacy of any actual democracy was emphasized by Max Weber in the course of his work, particularly in his political writings. In his view, the charisma of the statesman-political leader could contribute to the authority of democratic institutions. In this respect Harry Eckstein's thesis of congruence of authority patterns and the contribution that an authoritative leadership can make in a more authoritarian society— he refers specifically to the Kanzlerdemokratie in the German Federal Republic—is in the Weberian tradition.

17. The hypothesis that "the stability of a democratic system depends on both its *effectiveness* and its *legitimacy*, although these two concepts have often been confused in the concrete analysis of the crisis of a given political system," an elaboration of that distinction, and an application to some examples was first made by Lipset, emerging out of discussions with the author, in his essay "Political Sociology," in *Sociology Today: Problems and Prospects*, ed. Robert K. Merton, Leonard Broom, and Leonard S. Cottrell, Jr. (New York: Basic Books, 1959), pp. 81–114, esp. pp. 108–9. Lipset reiterated the point in *Political Man: the Social Bases of Politics*, (Garden City, N.Y.: Doubleday, 1960), chap. 3, pp. 77–98.

18. Leonardo Morlino, building on Eckstein, arrives at formulations very close to ours. He notes the need to distinguish decision-making efficacy from the capacity to implement decisions overcoming constraining conditions—to distinguish outputs from outcomes. In a footnote he even says: "The necessity to take into account [in the analysis] the outputs instead of the outcomes is another reason why we prefer decisional efficacy to effectiveness; effectiveness [effetività] tends to put the emphasis on the results. Our analysis makes efficacy and effectiveness separate variables in relation to the breakdown process, since they are not interchangeable or two dimensions of a single concept." See "Stabilità, legittimita e efficàcia decisionale nei sistèmi democràtici," *Rivista Italiana di Sciènza Politica* 3, no. 2 (August 1973):247–316, particularly pp. 280 ff.

Some time after I had written this analysis, someone called to my attention that Chester I. Barnard, in *The Functions of the Executive* (Cambridge, Mass.: Harvard University Press, 1947), pp. 19–20, used the terms "efficiency" and "effectiveness" to refer to a distinction similar to the one I had made between efficacy and effectiveness. I had read Barnard but was unaware of the following passage linking his work with mine:

> When a specific desired end is attained we shall say that the action is "effective." When the unsought consequences of the action are more important than the attainment of the desired end and are dissatisfactory, effective action, we shall say, is "inefficient." When the unsought consequences are unimportant or trivial, the action is "efficient." Moreover, it sometimes happens that the end sought is not attained, but the unsought consequences satisfy desires or motives not the "cause" of the action. We shall then regard such action as efficient but not effective. In retrospect the action in this case is justified not by the results sought but by those not sought. These observations are matters of common personal experience.
>
> Accordingly we shall say that an action is effective if it accomplishes its specific objective aim. We shall also say it is efficient if it satisfies the motives of that aim, whether it is effective or not, and the process does not create offsetting dissatisfactions. We shall say that an action is inefficient if the motives of that aim are not satisfied, or offsetting dissatisfactions are incurred, even if it is effective. This often occurs; we find we do not want what we thought we wanted.

19. Mancur Olson, *The Logic of Collective Action: Public Goods and the Theory of Groups* (Cambridge, Mass: Harvard University Press, 1965), pp. 132–33, 165–67, and 174–78.
20. The "function" or "purpose" of the state was a central theme in traditional political science—as the German literature on the *Staatszweck* shows. For a critical discussion, see Hermann Heller, *Staatslehre* (Leiden: A. W. Sijthoff's Uitgeversmaatschappij N.V., 1934). In a sense, the literature on "outputs" of the political system and on the role of the state in developing countries has replaced that approach, not always improving on earlier formulations.

    Since this essay was written, a new interest in problems close to our discussion of "unsolvable" problems has emerged around the questions of "overload of government" and "ungovernability." See the papers presented at the Colloquium on Overloaded Government, European University Institute, Florence, December 1976; Richard Rose, "Governing and Ungovernability: A Skeptical Inquiry," *Studies in Public Policy*, Centre for the Study of Public Policy, University of Strathclyde, Glasgow, 1977; and Erwin K. Scheuch, *Wird die Bundesrepublik unregierbar* (Cologne: Arbeitgeberverband der Metallindustrie, 1976).
21. Robert A. Dahl, *A Preface to Democratic Theory* (Chicago: University of Chicago Press, 1956), chap. 4, "Equality, Diversity, and Intensity," pp. 90–123.
22. Unfortunately, we have little data on how electorates and key elites perceive past regimes at different moments in time—immediately after their fall, in the course of the consolidation of a new regime, and with the passing of time—and how the performance of preceding regimes serves as frame of reference in the evaluation of new regimes. Social science should pay much more attention to what Maurice Halbwachs called *La Mémoire collective* (Paris: Presses universitaires de France, 1950).

    Since World War II, German survey research and an isolated study of Italian opinion have explored the image of past regimes. See G. R. Boynton and Gerhard Loewenberg, "The Decay of Support for Monarchy and the Hitler Regime in the Federal Republic of Germany," *British Journal of Political Science* 4 (1975):453–88, which relates those responses to satisfaction with the present regime.
23. Otto Kirchheimer, "Confining Conditions and Revolutionary Breakthroughs," *American Political Science Review* 59 (1965):964–74; the article has been anthologized in *Politics, Law and Social Change*, ed. Frederic S. Burin and Kurt L. Shell (New York: Columbia University Press, 1969).
24. Albert O. Hirschman, *Journeys toward Progress: Studies of Economic Policy-Making in Latin America* (Garden City, N.Y.: Doubleday, 1965), chap. 5, "The Continuing of Reform," pp. 327–84.
25. Albert O. Hirschman, "The Changing Tolerance for More Inequality in the Course of Economic Development; With a Mathematical Appendix by Michael Rothschild," *Quarterly Journal of Economics* 87 (November 1973):544–66.

26. Gabriel A. Almond and Sidney Verba, *The Civic Culture: Political Attitudes and Democracy in Five Nations* (Princeton, N.J.: Princeton University Press, 1963), is one of the outstanding exceptions. Steven F. Cohn, "Loss of Legitimacy and the Breakdown of Democratic Regimes: The Case of the Fourth Republic" (Ph.D. diss. Columbia University, 1976), is the first effort to test the questions raised here systematically with survey data collected over time under the Fourth Republic.

27. On this point see the discussion of "governmental inaction" by Charles Tilly in "Revolutions and Collective Violence," pp. 532–33, and Ted Robert Gurr, *Why Men Rebel* (Princeton, N.J.: Princeton University Press, 1969), pp. 235–36.

28. John F. Kennedy, in his speech on the Oxford, Mississippi, crisis. *New York Times,* 1 October 1962, p. 22.

29. Harry Eckstein, "On the Etiology of Internal Wars," *History and Theory* 4, no. 2 (1965):133–63, quotes Trotsky's list of the three elements necessary for revolution: "the political consciousness of the revolutionary class, the discontent of intermediate layers, and a ruling class which has lost faith in itself." Tilly, in "Revolutions and Collective Violence," in a list of four proximate conditions of revolution lists "incapacity or unwillingness of the agents of the government to suppress the alternative coalition or the commitment to its claims" (p. 521), and proceeds (pp. 532–37) to analyze "governmental inaction." The fate of the liberal state in Italy was certainly sealed when it tolerated—for whatever reasons (complicity or incapacity)—situations like those described by Renzo De Felice in *Mussolini il fascista, i Vol. I, La conquista del potere: 1921–1925* (Turin: Einaudi, 1966), pp. 25–30, 88–89, and 129. It was Fascist, Nazi, proletarian violence, which governments were partly unwilling and partly unable to check, that created a power vacuum leading to the breakdown. The Italian politician Salandra formulated it well when he wrote in a letter on 15 August 1922: "As you know I am, as you, both admiring and worried about fascism. Six years of weak and absent government, on occasion treasonous, have led us to put the hopes of the saving of the country in a force armed and organized outside of the powers of the State. This is a profoundly anarchic phenomenon in the strict sense of the word." See p. 286.
   On the other hand, Mussolini could comment to a fellow Fascist, G. Rossi: "If in Italy there were a government deserving that name today, without further delay it should send its agents and carabinieri to seal and occupy our offices. An organization armed with both cadres and a *Regolamento* [disciplinary code for its members] is inconceivable in a State that has its Army and its police. Therefore there is no state in Italy. It is useless; therefore, we have necessarily to come to power. Otherwise the history of Italy will become a *pochade* [an unfinished draft]." Ibid., p. 317. This was his response to the Facta government's failure to react to the provocation of institutionalizing a private army. Authority that is unwilling or unable to use force when challenged by force loses its claim to the obedience of even those not ready to question it. For them, authority may be prior to coercion, but for opponents like the *squadristi* the only resource left is effective coercion.

30. Pareto, *Mind and Society*, vol. 2, pp. 1527–28, no. 2186. To avoid the dangerous misinterpretation of Pareto as a mindless advocate of force, this text should be read in conjunction with numbers 2174 and 2175 (pp. 1512–13). In the context of our discussion it should be clear that those responsible for the maintenance of a democratic political order should be given, by those believing in the legitimacy of that order, the right to use adequate force to thwart opponents ready to use force to overthrow or to dislocate that order. The issue of coercion on the authorities or other citizens by political groups, the preparedness to do so, is not part of civil liberties, nor is the advocacy of such use by political leaders. Obviously such a rule must be applied without partisanship. A modern state cannot tolerate political groups, even those committed to democracy, defending themselves rather than being protected by the state.

31. Our excursus about the relationship between party systems and democratic stability is based on the extraordinarily insightful and stimulating typology of party systems and the analysis of their dynamics found in Giovanni Sartori, *Parties and Party Systems: A Framework for Analysis* (Cambridge: Cambridge University Press, 1976), vol. 1, chaps. 5 and 6, pp. 119–216.

32. Giuseppe Di Palma, *Surviving without Governing: The Italian Parties in Parliament* (Berkeley and Los Angeles: University of California Press, 1977), chaps. 6 and 7, pp. 219–86. For

the debate provoked by Sartori's application of his model of polarized multiparty systems to contemporary Italy, see his "Il caso italiano"; and Luciano Pellicani, "Verso il superamento del pluralismo polarizzato," in idem, pp. 645-74, where the reader will find other writings on the subject.

33. The idea of "dual sovereignty" implicit in Pareto's analysis was articulated by Leon Trotsky but also stated by Mussolini. On 4 October (less than a month before the March on Rome), he quoted with approval a newspaper analysis: "There are two governments in Italy today—one too many." Quoted in Christopher Seton-Watson, *Italy from Liberalism to Fascism: 1870-1925* (London: Methuen, 1967), p. 617. For an intelligent use of this notion of multiple sovereignty in the study of revolutions, see Tilly, "Revolutions and Collective Violence."

34. The whole problem of different types of opposition in democracies has been discussed in Robert A. Dahl's contributions to *Political Oppositions in Western Democracies* (New Haven: Yale University Press, 1966), and his *Polyarchy*.

35. Richard Rose, *Governing without Consensus: An Irish Perspective* (Boston: Beacon Press, 1971). See particularly chap. 5, "How People View the Regime," pp. 179-202, and chap. 7, "Party Allegiance," pp. 218-246. See also Arend Lijphart, "The Northern Ireland Problem: Cases, Theories, and Solutions," *British Journal of Political Science* 5 (1975):83-106. See also Richard Rose, *Northern Ireland: Time of Choice* (Washington, D.C.: American Enterprise Institute, 1976), and idem, "On the Priorities of Citizenship in the Deep South and Northern Ireland," *Journal of Politics* 38 (1976):247-91.

When permanent, numerically weak minorities of distinctive cultural, racial, national, and religious characteristics are confronted with a majority that rejects cooperation with them, then the rights of that minority are not likely to be protected, nor are its interests taken into account by the rule "one man, one vote." (This is particularly true with single-member, majority representation.) In this case all the formal elements of democracy may exist, but the spirit may be violated or absent. Rose argues that in such a situation equality before the courts, and the enforcement of legal rights by them, might be a better avenue than the vote to the benefits of citizenship.

36. In this context, Roth, *Social Democrats in Imperial Germany*, is particularly relevant. For the concept of negative integration, see pp. 311-22.

37. A prime example would be the convergence of the Nazis and the Communists in parliamentary opposition to the Weimar parties, which made the "system" unworkable. A more concrete example would be the strike of the Berlin city transport workers in 1932, initiated, against the decision of the trade unions, by the Nazis and Communists, who turned to sabotage and violence. This strike had an important psychological impact on the thinking of the *Reichswehr* and its planning for a two-pronged attack. See Hans Otto Meissner and Harry Wilde, *Die Machtergreifung: Ein Bericht über die Technik des Nationalsozialistischen Staatsstreiches* (Stuttgart: Cotta'sche Buchhandlung, 1958), pp. 11-20, for an account of those events. On the policy of the KPD, see Hermann Weber, *Die Wandlung des deutschen Kommunismus: Die Stalinisierung der KPD in der Weimarer Republik* (Frankfurt: Europäische Verlagsanstalt, 1969). On the *Reichswehr* reaction, see Francis L. Carsten, *Reichswehr und Politik, 1918-1933* (Cologne: Kiepenheuer and Witsch, 1964), pp. 429 ff.

38. This is not to deny that such forces do not play a role in politics, but they certainly do not operate to the extent and in the way they are alleged to do in such simplified conspiratorial interpretations of politics. For an outstanding analysis of this style of politics, see Seymour M. Lipset and Earl Raab, *The Politics of Unreason: Right-Wing Extremism in America, 1790-1970* (New York: Harper and Row, 1970). Extremists, themselves prone to conspiratorial activities, infiltration, manipulation of causes, and untruthful propaganda, are likely to project their behavior onto their opponents. The danger point is reached when such beliefs become shared by more moderate, Establishment types, as when Attorney General Brownell abetted the labeling of the Democratic party with treason in the heyday of McCarthyism.

39. On the French crisis in 1958, see Cohn, "Losses of Legitimacy," which developed ideas originally presented at the World Congress of Sociology in Varna, Bulgaria, in 1970. This monograph tests many of the hypotheses of this chapter, including a sophisticated analysis of the available survey data collected by the IFOP.

Scandals occupy a special place in French politics and have contributed considerably to the delegitimation of politicians, parties, Parliament, and the Third and Fourth Republics. For an insightful analysis of the functions and dynamics of scandals (very applicable to the Spanish crisis in 1935), see Philip Williams, "The Politics of Scandal," in *Wars, Plots, and Scandals in Post-War France* (Cambridge: Cambridge University Press, 1970), pp. 3–16. For a review of the literature on the May 1958 crisis, see idem, pp. 129–66.

40. On the Italian perception of the Communist party, see Juan J. Linz, "La democrazìa italiana di fronte al futuro," in *Il caso italiano: Italia anni 70*, ed. Fabio Luca Cavazza and Stephen R. Graubard (Milano: Garzanti, 1974), pp. 124–62. See esp. p. 161, which also refers to comparable French data. Also see Giacomo Sani, "Mass Constraints on Coalition Realignments: Images of Anti-System Parties in Italy," *British Journal of Political Science* 5, (January 1976):1–32, and "Mass Level Response to Party Strategy: The Italian Electorate and the Communist Party," in *Communism in Italy and France*, ed. Donald L. Blackmer and Sidney Tarrow (Princeton, N.J.: Princeton University Press, 1975), pp. 456–544.

41. See chapter by Risto Alapuro and Erik Allardt, "The Lapua Movement: The Threat of Rightist Takeover in Finland, 1930–32," in this volume.

42. The danger of identifying the regime with the policies of the first majority that instored it is well stated by Gil Robles:

> Against whom has national opinion voted? Has it voted against the regime or against its policy? For me, honestly, at least today, the Spanish people has voted against the policy of the Constituent Assembly. However, if you, who have in your hands the governing of the state, you who militate in the opposition, insist in identifying, as until now, the policy followed with the regime; if you attempt to convince the Spanish people that socialism, sectarianism and Republic are consubstantial, then you can rest assured that the people will vote against the Republic and the regime. In that hypothesis it shall not be us who shall oppose the sweeping march of Spanish opinion.

Quoted in Carlos Seco Serrano, "La experiencia de la derecha posibilista en la Segunda república española: Estudio preliminar," in José María Gil Robles, *Discursos parlamentarios* (Madrid: Taurus, 1971), xxxiii–xxxiv.

43. Rose, "Dynamic Tendencies in the Authority of Regimes."

44. The relationship between government-cabinet stability or instability and regime stability needs further exploration. Recently, considerable attention has been paid to a more systematic measurement of cabinet instability and the analysis of its causes. See, for example, Hurwitz, "An Index of Democratic Political Stability," and Michael Taylor and V. M. Herman, "Party Systems and Government Stability," *American Political Science Review* 65 (1971):28–37. Klaus von Beyme, *Die parlamentarischen Regierungssysteme in Europa* (Munich: R. Piper, 1970), presents data on cabinet instability in a number of European countries since the nineteenth century and its causes; see pp. 875–84 and 901–67. An excellent monograph on the subject is A. Soulier, *L'instabilité ministériele sous la Troisième République (1871–1938)* (Paris: Recueil Sirey, 1939).

We have some systematic evidence that cabinet instability is closely related to the breakdown of European parliamentary democracies in the interwar years, and to the intensity of the crises. Obviously, this is not a cause-and-effect relationship, since government instability is a reflection of the political and social crisis, but we have little doubt that frequent changes in government also contribute to that crisis. Data to support this contention are found in the table on p. 111. Taking the average duration of interwar cabinets before the depression and after it (a measure that has its limitations and could be refined), we see that in only one of the countries in which governments lasted less than nine months on the average did democracy survive, and that was France. On the other hand, within that group of countries in which governments lasted longer than nine months, only one experienced a regime change. That was Estonia, with its preemptive authoritarianism in which a democratically elected leader broke with democratic legality in a crisis situation. In most of the countries that had stable governments before the depression—the Netherlands, the United Kingdom, Denmark, Sweden, Norway, and Ireland—all of whom had governments with an average duration of one year or more, the postdepression governments were more stable. (This did not hold true for the Netherlands, the second most stable, where the duration dropped from 996 days to 730.) Even in Finland, which faced a serious crisis, stability

Cabinet Instability in European Parliamentary Systems between World War I and World War II or the Breakdown of Democracy

| | Predepression | |
Country	Dates Covered	Average Duration (in days)
Portugal	16 May 1918–28 May 1926	117
	30 cabinets, 19 prime ministers	
Yugoslavia	? December 1918–? January 1929	154
	24 cabinets, 7 prime ministers	
Spain	21 March 1918–13 September 1923	166
	12 cabinets, 7 prime ministers	
Germany	9 November 1918–27 March 1930	210
	18 cabinets, 9 prime ministers	
France	16 November 1917–3 November 1929	239
	18 cabinets, 8 prime ministers	
Italy	30 October 1917–30 October 1922	260
	7 cabinets, 5 prime ministers	
Austria	30 October 1918–30 September 1930	267
	16 cabinets, 6 prime ministers	
Finland	17 April 1919–4 July 1930	294
	14 cabinets, 12 prime ministers	
Estonia	25 January 1921–2 July 1929	306
	10 cabinets, 7 prime ministers	
Czechoslovakia	14 September 1918–7 December 1929	340
	12 cabinets, 7 prime ministers	
Ireland	? January 1919–? March 1932	368
	10 cabinets, 5 prime ministers	
Belgium	31 May 1918–6 June 1931	432
	11 cabinets, 7 prime ministers	
Norway	31 January 1913–12 May 1931	441
	9 cabinets, 8 prime ministers	
Sweden	19 October 1917–7 June 1930	461
	10 cabinets, 8 prime ministers	
Denmark	30 March 1920–30 April 1929	533
	6 cabinets, 5 prime ministers	
United Kingdom	10 January 1919–5 November 1931	668
	7 cabinets, 4 prime ministers	
Netherlands	9 September 1918–10 August 1929	996
	4 cabinets, 3 prime ministers	
	Postdepression	
Portugal	—	—
Yugoslavia	—	—
Spain	14 April 1931–18 July 1936	101
	19 cabinets, 8 prime ministers	
Germany	30 March 1930–30 January 1933	258
	4 cabinets, 3 prime ministers	
France	3 November 1929–16 June 1940	165
	22 cabinets, 13 prime ministers	
Italy	—	—
Austria	30 September 1930–20 May 1932	149
	4 cabinets, 4 prime ministers	
Finland	4 July 1930–27 March 1940	592
	6 cabinets, 6 prime ministers	
Estonia	9 July 1929–17 October 1933	260
	6 cabinets, 5 prime ministers	

Cabinet Instability in European Parliamentary Systems between World War I and World War II or the Breakdown of Democracy (cont.)

	Predepression	
Country	*Dates Covered*	*Average Duration (in days)*
Czechoslovakia	7 December 1929–5 October 1938	537
	6 cabinets, 4 prime ministers	
Ireland	? March 1932–? June 1938	750
	3 cabinets, 1 prime minister	
Belgium	6 June 1931–22 February 1939	285
	11 cabinets, 11 prime ministers	
Norway	12 May 1931–25 June 1945	469
	4 cabinets, 4 prime ministers	
Sweden	7 June 1930–13 December 1939	694
	5 cabinets, 5 prime ministers	
Denmark	30 April 1929–4 May 1942	4750
	1 cabinet, 1 prime minister	
United Kingdom	5 November 1931–28 May 1940	1035
	3 cabinets, 3 prime ministers	
Netherlands	10 August 1929–9 August 1939	730
	5 cabinets, 2 prime ministers	

NOTE: The number of days cannot be considered exact, since it is not always clear precisely when a government falls and another is constituted. Another measure of instability would be the number of days taken to form a new government.

increased. It was only in Belgium that the duration dropped closer to the danger point: from 432 days to 285.

45. The question of the relationship between democratic stability and electoral systems has been the object of prolonged and intense debate since Ferdinand A. Hermens launched his blistering attack on the destructive implications of proportional representation with *Democracy or Anarchy*? (Notre Dame, Ind.: Notre Dame University Press, 1941). Maurice Duverger, with his classic work, *Political Parties* (New York: John Wiley, 1963), Anthony Downs, with *The Economic Theory of Democracy* (New York: Harper, 1957), and the numerous writings of Giovanni Sartori (see nn. 13, 16, and 68) and the polemics surrounding them, have all contributed to the argument. The most important monograph is Douglas W. Rae, *The Political Consequences of Electoral Laws* (New Haven: Yale University Press, 1971). Stein Sparre Nilson, "Wahlsoziologische Probleme des Nationalsozialismus," *Zeitschrift für die gesamte Staatswissenschaft* 60, no. 2 (1954): 282–83, illustrates the complexity of the problem. The case of Weimar has been analyzed in great detail in Hans Fenske's monograph, *Wahlrecht und Parteiensystem: Ein Beitrag zur deutschen Parteiengeschichte* (Frankfurt: Athenäeum, 1972). See also Friedrich Schäfer, "Zur Frage des Wahlrechts in der Weimarer Republik," in *Staat, Wirtschaft, und Politik in der Weimarer Republik: Festschrift für Heinrich Brüning*, ed. Ferdinand A. Hermens and Theodor Schieder (Berlin: Duncker and Humblot, 1967), pp. 119–40, particularly on the debates and proposals for election law reform in the face of the impending crisis. The theoretical refinements and empirical analysis of different cases make it questionable to put all the blame on proportional representation, since a majority system can lead to equally destructive consequences in a polarized society with large extremist minorities. Much depends on the point in the crystallization of the party system at which one or another electoral system is introduced.

46. Werner Kaltefleiter, *Wirtschaft und Politik in Deutschland: Konjunktur als Bestimmungfaktor des Parteiensystems* (Cologne: Westdeutscher Verlag, 1968). See also Heinrich Bennecke, *Wirtschaftliche Depression und politischer Radikalismus, 1918–1938* (Munich: Olzog, 1970), who, in addition to Germany, refers to Austria and the Sudetenland.

47. Karl Dietrich Bracher, "The Technique of the National Socialist Seizure of Power," in *The Path to Dictatorship, 1918–1933: Ten Essays by German Scholars* (Garden City, N.Y.: Doubleday, 1966), pp. 113–32. See esp. p. 117. See also idem, *Die Auflösung der Weimarer Republik: Eine Studie zum Problem des Machtverfalls in der Demokratie* (Stuttgart: Ring 1957); idem, *The German Dictatorship* (New York: Praeger 1970); and idem, with Wolfgang Sauer and Gerhard Schulz, *Die nationalsozialistische Machtergreifung: Studien zur Errichtung des totalitären Herrschaftssystems in Deutschland, 1933–34* (Cologne: Westdeutscher Verlag, 1960).

48. See also his contribution to this work; *The Military in Politics*; "The New Professionalism of Internal Warfare and Military Role Expansion," in *Authoritarian Brazil: Origins, Policies, and Future*, ed. Alfred Stepan (New Haven: Yale University Press, 1973), pp. 47–65; *The State and Society: Peru in Comparative Perspective* (Princeton, N.J.: Princeton University Press, 1978). See also John S. Fitch, *The Military Coup d'Etat as a Conservative Political Process: Ecuador, 1948–1966* (Baltimore: Johns Hopkins University Press, 1977).

49. Charles Tilly, "Does Modernization Breed Revolution?" *Comparative Politics* 3 (April 1973):447.

50. The change of the national flag by the German and Spanish republics provided an opportunity for such conflicts. Another example is the substitution of *Viva la República* for *Viva España* in official and army ceremonies.

51. *Ressentiment* has been the object of an interesting monograph by the philosopher-sociologist Max Scheler, entitled *Ressentiment* (New York: Free Press of Glencoe, 1961) (edited and with an Introduction by Lewis A. Coser). The term was derived from Nietzsche, in whose work it occupies a central place and is the object of a phenomenological description. Coser's summary follows (to retain the distinctive meaning of the word, the French spelling used by Nietzsche and Scheler has been used rather than the English word "resentment"):

> It denotes an attitude which arises from a cumulative repression of feelings of hatred, revenge, envy and the like. When such feelings can be acted out, no *ressentiment* results. But when a person is unable to release the feelings against the persons or groups evoking them, thus developing a sense of impotence, and when these feelings are continuously re-experienced over time, then *ressentiment* arises. *Ressentiment* leads to a tendency to degrade, to reduce genuine values as well as their bearers. As distinct from rebellion, *ressentiment* does not lead to an affirmation of countervalues since *ressentiment*-imbued persons secretly crave the values they publicly denounce (p. 24).

Typically, ressentiment politics is more anti-something than pro-something.

52. For examples, see Carmelo Lisón-Tolosana, *Belmonte de los Caballeros: A Sociological Study of a Spanish Town* (Oxford: The Clarendon Press, 1966), pp. 45, 289–90.

53. Robert E. Lane, *The Regulation of Businessmen: Social Conditions of Government Economic Control* (New Haven: Yale University Press, 1954), has emphasized the psychological rather than material cost of regulation and resistance to it. See pp. 19–35.

54. It is obviously difficult to gauge the impact of the Versailles treaty, its different provisions, the reparation agreements, and the interventions of the Allies, particularly the Ruhr occupation, on internal political developments, but they cannot have been negligible. See Erich Matthias, "The Influence of the Versailles Treaty on the Internal Development of the Weimar Republic," in *German Democracy and the Triumph of Hitler*, ed. Anthony Nicholls and Erich Matthias (London: Georg Allen and Unwin, 1971), pp. 13–28. For evidence in the autobiographies of Nazi activists, see Merkl, *Political Violence under the Swastika*, passim.

55. See the chapter by Paolo Farneti in this volume.

56. See Guillermo A. O'Donnell, *Modernization and Bureaucratic-Authoritarianism: Studies in South American Politics* (Berkeley, Ca.: Institute of International Studies, 1973), chap. 4, "An Impossible 'Game': Party Competition in Argentina, 1955-1966," pp. 166–99.

57. The implications of different degrees of continuity or discontinuity in the political elite after changes in regime, particularly democratization, have not been studied. See Juan J. Linz, "Continuidad y discontinuidad en la elite política española: De la Restauración el Régimen actual," in *Estudios de Ciencia Política y Sociología: Homenaje al Profesor Carlos Ollero* (Madrid: Carlavilla, 1972), pp. 361–424.

58. Pareto, *Mind and Society*.

59. We are referring to his development of the concept, coined by Alfred Weber, of "socially unattached intelligentsia" [freischwebende Intelligenz]. Karl Mannheim, *Ideology and Utopia: An Introduction to the Sociology of Knowledge* (New York: Harcourt Brace Jovanovich, n.d.), pp. 153–64.

60. There has been no comparative study of the role of intellectuals in the crises of pluralistic democracies; and it is often assumed, in view of their persecution or rejection by authoritarian or totalitarian regimes succeeding them, that they must have been identified with the overthrown democratic state. Only in the case of Germany has the role of intellectuals—those influential among both the elites and the mass public—been the object of considerable research and polemic. See Peter Gay, *Weimar Culture: The Outsider as Insider* (New York: Harper and Row, 1968), and the issue of *Social Research* entitled *Germany 1919–1932: The Weimar Culture* (vol. 39, no. 2, Summer 1972). George Mosse, *The Crisis of German Ideology: Intellectual Origins of the Third Reich* (New York: Grosset and Dunlop, 1964), has rightly paid special attention to the broad penetration of völkisch antiWeimar ideologies through a multitude of channels. Nor should we forget the debunking of the Weimar system and the Social Democrats by the leftist intelligentsia. See Istvan Deak, *Weimar Germany's Left-Wing Intellectuals* (Berkeley and Los Angeles: University of California Press, 1969).

No similar analyses exist for Italy and Spain. Certainly the intellectual critique, as Salvemini recognized in his Foreword to William Salomone, *Italian Democracy in the Making*, contributed to the alienation from Giolittian Italy. In Spain, leading intellectuals like Ortega y Gasset, Unamuno, and others had a short honeymoon with the Republic, then turned highly critical (see my chapter on Spain in this volume). Fortunately, the work by Alastair Hamilton, *The Appeal of Fascism* (New York: Avon, 1971) (with a Foreword by Stephen Spender), has corrected the misleading impression that only second-rate intellectuals and writers could be found supporting or toying with Fascism even when anti-Fascists predominated at later stages. Unfortunately, cultural critics of both the Right and the Left contributed, often irresponsibly, often by expressions of sympathy for movements they did not know well, to the undermining of imperfect, but nevertheless civil democratic, polities.

Few texts reveal the ambivalence toward freedom of many intellectuals as well as these words written in 1931:

> The notion of liberty such as it is taught us, seems to me false and pernicious in the extreme. And if I approve Soviet constraint I must also approve Fascist discipline. I believe ever more firmly that the idea of liberty is nothing but a hoax. I would like to be sure that I would think the same if I were not free myself, I who value my own liberty of thought above all else: but I also believe more and more firmly that man does nothing valid without constraint, and that those capable of finding this constraint within themselves are very rare. I believe, too, that the true color of a particular thought only assumes its full value when it is thrown into relief against an unperturbed background. It is the uniformity of the masses which enables certain individuals to rise up and stand out against it. The "Render unto Caesar the things which are Caesar's; and unto God the things that are God's" of the Gospel seems to me wiser than ever. On God's side we have liberty—the liberty of the spirit; on Caesar's side there is submission—the submission of our acts. (André Gide, *Journal, 1889–1939*, quoted in Hamilton, *Appeal of Fascism*, p. 24.)

A perfect example would be Oswald Spengler, writing "Hitler is a fool, but one must support his movement," voting for him and displaying Swastika flags with the explanation that "When one has a chance to annoy people, one should do so." Hamilton, *Appeal of Fascism*, p. 174.

61. Kelsen, *Vom Wesen und Wert der Demokratie*, and "Foundations of Democracy." There is certainly a tension between "ideology" as a belief system based on fixed elements, and characterized by strong affect and closed cognitive structure, and its converse, "pragmatism," as these terms are defined by Giovanni Sartori in "Politics, Ideology, and Belief Systems," *American Political Science Review* 63 (June 1969):398–411. It might be argued that the unconditional commitment to democratic constitutional procedures, defense of the civil liberties required for their continuous operation, and the rejection of extra-legal violence against legitimate authorities are also ideological.

CHAPTER 3

1. The emphasis on confining conditions is Otto Kirchheimer's contribution to our analysis. See his "Confining Conditions and Revolutionary Breakthroughs."
2. Albert Hirschman has highlighted those social and psychological processes, particularly in *Journeys toward Progress* (Garden City, N.Y.: Doubleday, Anchor Books, 1965) chap. 4, "Problem-solving and Policy-making: A Latin American Style?" pp. 299–326.
3. Karl von Clausewitz, *War, Politics, and Power*, ed. Edward M. Collins (Chicago: Regnery, 1962), pp. 83, 92–93, and 254–63. (This volume consists of selections from *On War* and *I Believe and Profess*.)
4. Max Weber, "Science as a Vocation," in *From Max Weber: Essays in Sociology*, ed. Hans H. Gerth and C. Wright Mills (New York: Oxford University Press, 1958), pp. 129–56; see esp. pp. 156–62.
5. The bind in which Social Democrats found themselves was well described by Fritz Tarnow, deputy and head of the Woodworker's Union, in the key address at the last SPD party convention (1931) before the rise of Hitler, when he said: "Do we stand . . . at the sick-bed of capitalism merely as the diagnostician, or also as the doctor who seeks to cure? Or as joyous heirs, who can hardly wait for the end and would even like to help it along with poison? . . . It seems to me that we are condemned both to be the doctor who earnestly seeks to cure and at the same time to retain the feeling that we are the heirs, who would prefer to take over the entire heritage of the capitalist system today rather than tomorrow." Quoted in Franz Neumann, *Behemoth: The Structure and Practice of National Socialism, 1933–1944* (New York: Octagon, 1963), p. 31. It was characterized by the Italian Claudio Treves in March 1920 in these words: "This is the tragedy of the present crisis: you can no longer impose your order on us, and we cannot yet impose ours on you." Quoted by Seton-Watson in *Italy from Liberalism to Fascism*, p. 560. See also the quote from Turati on p. 559.
6. Max Weber noted that German parties in the Bismarckian empire, excluded from actual control of the executive and therefore from full responsibility, tended to be highly ideological or closely identified with specific interest groups. Many parties therefore got into the habit, which continued in the Weimar Republic, of acting more like pressure groups than parties. The leadership struggle in the German DNVP between Hugenberg and Graf Westarp and of Lord Beaverbrook and Baldwin in the British Conservative party had different outcomes that reflect this difference. See Weber, "Parliament and Government in a Reconstructed Germany," in *Economy and Society*, ed. Guenther Roth and Claus Wittich (New York: Bedminster Press, 1968), vol. 3, pp. 1381–1469. See esp. pp. 1392, 1409, 1424–30, and 1448.
7. This process was decisive in weakening German bourgeois and rural-based parties in the last years of the Weimar Republic and in the success of Nazism both electorally and in gaining access to the Establishment. Another aspect is the veto by interest groups—business or trade unions—of decisions of parties and party leaders running counter to their interests even when *political* considerations—the concern for the stability of the system—demanded sacrifices. The rigidity of the trade unions in relation to the SPD and of business interests in relation to the DVP contributed decisively to the fall of the Müller cabinet, the last parliamentary government of Weimar. See Helga Timm, *Die deutsche Sozialpolitik und der Bruch der Grossen Koalition im März 1930*, Beiträge zur Geschichte des Parlamentarismus und der politischen Parteien, no. 1 (Düsseldorf: Droste, 1953).
8. Quoted in Joachim C. Fest, *The Face of the Third Reich: Portraits of Nazi Leadership* (New York: Pantheon Books, 1970), n. 25.
9. See Hirschman, *Journeys toward Progress*, pt. 2, "Problem-solving and Reformmongering," which is one of the most stimulating analyses of policy-making I know. Rather than review here many of its propositions—directly relevant to our analysis—I urge the reader to turn to this work.
10. Philip M. Williams, *Crisis and Compromise: Politics in the Fourth Republic* (Hamden, Conn.: Archon, 1964), pp. 426–27, notes that, "obliged to face the facts they hoped to dodge, politicians repeatedly conceded to a new premier the very demands on which they had overthrown his predecessor.... All too frequently a year with no crisis meant a year of no policy, and the continued presence of a group of ministers distracted attention from the

absence of government." The crisis was also a decision-making device," a method of government by shock treatment."

11. This is a central theme in the work of this political scientist, who was an insightful observer of and participant in the breakdown of Weimar democracy. In his decisionistic view of the political process and in his 1927 definition of politics in terms of the *Freund-Feind* ("friend-enemy") distinction, he reflected the "incivil" politics of his time. See Mathias Schmitz, *Die Freund-Feind-Theorie Carl Schmitts* (Cologne: Westdeutscher Verlag, 1965), for a discussion and references to Carl Schmitt's writings and secondary sources.

12. See nn. 46 and 83.

13. Albert O. Hirschman, *Exit, Voice, and Loyalty* (Cambridge, Mass: Harvard University Press, 1970), p. 91.

14. The term "crisis strata" was coined by Sigmund Neumann in *Permanent Revolution: Totalitarianism in the Age of International Civil War* (New York: Praeger, 1965) pp. 30-32, 106-11. This is not the place to refer to the extensive literature on social movements and the conditions for their emergence and success. For a recent review, see Anthony Oberschall, *Social Conflict and Social Movements* (Englewood Cliffs, N.J.: Prentice-Hall, 1973). Since Fascist movements played a major role in the breakdown or crises of democracies studied here, but a sociologico-historical analysis of Fascism falls outside of the scope we have set to our essay, the reader is referred to Juan J. Linz, "Some Notes toward a Comparative Study of Fascism in Sociological Historical Prespective," in *A Reader's Guide to Fascism*, ed. Walter Laqueur (Berkeley and Los Angeles: University of California Press, 1976), pp. 3-121, as well as other essays in that volume.

15. Curt Erich Suckert [Curzio Malaparte], *Coup d'Etat: The Technique of Revolution* (New York: E. P. Dutton, 1932).

16. Gurr, *Why Men Rebel*, Hugh Davis Graham and Ted Robert Gurr, eds. *Violence in America: Historical and Comparative Perspectives* (Washington, D.C.: National Commission on the Causes and Prevention of Violence, 1969); Robert M. Fogelson, *Violence as Protest: A Study of Riots and Ghettos* (Garden City, N.Y. Doubleday, 1971); and H. L. Nieburg, *Political Violence: The Behavioral Process* (New York: St. Martin's Press, 1969).

17. This was particularly true under the Weimar Republic, where acts of violence and assassinations by rightist patriotic "idealists" were treated with incredible leniency, while similar actions by leftist "revolutionaries" were harshly punished. This certainly undermined the legitimacy of the legal order and the political system. See Gumbel, *Vom Fememord zur Reichskanzlei;* Heinrich E. Hannover and Elisabeth Hannover, *Politische Justiz, 1918-1933* (Frankfurt: Fischer, 1966); and Bracher, *Die Auflösung der Weimarer Republik*, pp. 191-98. This attitude of the judiciary was also reflected in its decisions in constitutional matters in favor of authoritarian solutions.

In Italy, too, the authorities, particularly the lower echelons of the police, were far from neutral in their response to political violence. This point is well documented by reports of prefects like Mori, who wanted to preserve the authority of the state; it is also reflected in the statistics compiled by the Ministry of the Interior. For example, of 1073 acts of violence committed on 8 May 1921, 964 had been denounced to the judicial authority by the parties. But the most telling fact is that 396 Fascists had been arrested and 878 allowed to go free, while 1421 Socialists were arrested and 617 allowed to go free. See De Felice, *Mussolini il fascista*, vol. 1, pp. 35 and passim. The great Socialist historian Gaetano Salvemini has effectively described the resultant climate of violence and its origins.

We have no systematic data on the behavior of the judiciary in the Spanish crisis, but the fact that both the Right and later the Left had plans to introduce reforms making it more dependent on the government suggests that it might have been more impartial. Even so, the slowness of proceedings contributed indirectly to political tension, since it meant unnecessary detentions, as Joaquín Chapaprieta, who was prime minister in 1935, noted in *La paz fue posible* (Esplugues de Llobregat: Ariel, 1971), pp. 378-80. In this case we find the complaint that the courts tended to be lenient with "social crimes."

18. To capture the atmosphere created by the presence of paramilitary organizations of parties, see the excellent monograph by William Sheridan Allen, *The Nazi Seizure of Power: The Experience of a Single German Town, 1930-1935* (Chicago: Quadrangle, 1965), and the

many local histories of the rise to power of the Italian Fascists and the struggle against them. For a "collective biography" of such activists and streetfighters, see Merkl, *Political Violence under the Swastika*, based on autobiographies volunteered by Nazis in response to an appeal by sociologist Theodor Abel.

19. On the paramilitary organizations emerging in the period after World War I, their variety, ideologies and transformation in the course of the Republic, see Bracher, *Die Auflösung der Weimarer Republik*, chap. 5, and the older studies by Ernst H. Posse, *Die politischen Kampfbünde Deutschlands* (Berlin, 1931), and Robert G. L. Waite, *Vanguard of Nazism: The Free Corps Movement in Postwar Germany, 1918–1923* (Cambridge, Mass: Harvard University Press, 1952). See also Wolfgang Abendroth, "Zur Geschichte des Roten Frontkämpferbundes," in *Dem Verleger Anton Hain Zum 75: Geburtstag am 4. Mai 1967*, ed. Alwien Diemer (Meisenheim: Glan, 1967). For Italy, see Giovanni Sabbatucci, *I combattènti nel primo dopoguerra* (Bari: Laterza, 1974), and Fernando Cordova, *Arditi e Legionari d' annunziani*, (Padova: Marsilio, 1969). For a general analysis, see Michael A. Ledeen, "The War as a Style of Life," in *The War Generation*, ed. Stephen Ward (New York: Kennikat, 1975).

20. For Austria, see Bruce Frederick Pauley, "Hahnenschwanz and Swastika: The Styrian Heimatschutz and Austrian National Socialism, 1918-1934" (PH.D. diss., University of Rochester, 1967), and Ludwig Jedlicka, "The Austrian Heimwehr," *Journal of Contemporary History* 1, no. 1 (1966):127-44.

21. See Allan Mitchell, *Revolution in Bavaria 1918-1919: The Eisner Regime and the Soviet Republic* (Princeton, N.J.: Princeton University Press, 1965). Werner T. Angress, *Stillborn Revolution: The Communist Bid for Power in Germany, 1921-1923* (Princeton, N.J.: Princeton University Press, 1963), is another monograph on the early assaults of the Left against German democracy.

22. Since democracy and nationalism were "born" together in the historical sense, and the first successful democracies were nation-states (with the exception of the Swiss confederation of democratic cantons), theorists made little effort to deal with the possible conflict between national aspirations and democratic politics. Democracy was in fact identified with national sovereignty. Only with the democratization of the Austro-Hungarian Empire and the application of Wilsonian principles of national self-determination did the problem become visible, but the anti- or ademocratic politics in Eastern Europe soon obscured it again. Even the appearance of multinational states in the Third World and the resurgence of primordial ethnic identities in recent years in Western Europe have not yet led to a systematic analysis, except in the framework of the literature on consociational democracies. The renewed interest in linguistic and cultural conflict has led to interesting analyses of individual countries but no systematic studies of how to guarantee the rights of minorities and how to handle the problems of secession, which received some attention in the twenties and thirties.

The tension had already been recognized by Lord Acton when he wrote:

The greatest adversary of the rights of nationality is the modern theory of nationality. By making the State and the nation commensurate with each other in theory, it reduces practically to a subject condition all other nationalities that may be within the boundary. It cannot admit them to an equality with the ruling nation which constitutes the State, because the State would then cease to be national, which would be a contradiction of the principle of its existence. According, therefore, to the degree of humanity and civilization in that dominant body which claims all the rights of the community, the inferior races are exterminated, or reduced to servitude, or outlawed, or put in a condition of dependence. *(Essays on Freedom and Power* [Boston: Beacon, 1948], p. 192.)

23. This is not the place to refer to the extensive literature on communal conflict and civil wars of secession. A case where formal democratic institutions have not worked rather than broken down is that of Northern Ireland. At the Varna sessions Richard Rose presented a paper on that case that has not been included in this volume, since he published an extensive analysis in *Governing without Consensus*. See also Lijphart, "The Northern Ireland Problem."

For evidence on the small number of multilingual democracies, see Joshua A. Fishman,

"Some Contrasts between Linguistically Homogeneous and Linguistically Heterogeneous Polities," in *Language Problems of Developing Nations,* ed. Joshua A. Fishman, Charles A. Ferguson, and Jyatirindra das Gupta (New York: Wiley, 1968). See also Eric Nordlinger, *Conflict Regulation in Divided Societies*, Harvard University Center for International Affairs, Occassional Paper no. 29 (Cambridge, Mass., 1972), which focuses on the most constructive attempts to regulate conflict. Alvin Rabushka and Kenneth A. Shepsle, *Politics in Plural Societies: A Theory of Democratic Instability* (Columbus, Ohio: Charles E. Merrill, 1972), is a most pessimistic account, with reference to many countries, of the possibility for stable democracy in plural societies.

24. K. D. McRae *Consociational Democracy;* idem, "The Concept of Consociational Democracy and Its Application to Canada," in *Les états multilingues: Problèmes et solutions,* ed. Jean-Guy Savard and Richard Vigneault (Quebec: Université Laval, 1975), pp. 245–301.

25. It is significant that in our time social scientists have been writing about "nation-building" when the task in most parts of the world is "state-building." Similarly, the idea of patriotism, which did not imply a nationalistic sense of identity, has disappeared from our language. In this context the work of Robert Michels, *Der Patriotismus: Prolegomena zu seiner soziologischen Analyse* (Munich: Duncker and Humblot, 1929), still deserves attention.

26. Joshua Fishman, "Bilingualism with and without Diglossia: Diglossia with or without Bilingualism," *Journal of Social Issues* 23 (1967):29–38.

27. See Savard and Vigneault, *Les états multilingues*, for a number of papers relevant to the problem. There is obviously one notable exception: Switzerland. See Jürg Steiner, *Amicable Agreement versus Majority Rule: Conflict Resolution in Switzerland* (Chapel Hill: University of North Carolina Press, 1974). Other exceptions are Belgium, Canada, possibly India, and until recently, Lebanon.

28. See Walter Simon's chapter on Austria in *The Breakdown of Democratic Regimes: Europe.*

29. The imbalances in power between Prussia and the Reich, the particularistic policies of Bavaria that contributed to a crisis like the Beer Hall Putsch, the opportunity for the Nazis to enter Land governments like Thuringia, and the divergent policies of Land authorities in the defense of the state against paramilitary organizations all contributed to the exacerbation of the crisis. See, for example, Ernst-August Roloff, *Bürgertum und Nationalsocialismus, 1930–1933: Braunschweigs Weg ins Dritte Reich* (Hannover: Verlag für Literatur und Zeitgeschehen, 1961.)

30. The Germans even invented a term for those attempts—*Zähmungskonzept* [conceptions of domestication]. Those attempts at the cooptation of a well-organized opponent, one who is often in control of the street, inevitably led the opposition to "ask for more and more." In this case Clemenceau's statement that "Every man or every power whose action consists solely in surrender can only finish by self-annihilation. Everything that lives resists..." (quoted by Eckstein in "Etiology of Internal Wars," p. 157) became only too true. What was conceived as containment led to appeasement and finally to surrender. Examples of this process of negotiation, generally covert and done through intermediaries, can be found in De Felice, *Mussolini il fascista,* Vol. 1, pp. 255–60, 282–85, 300–305, and 345–46. Such negotiation was based on the growing conviction among the elite that "Contra il fascismo oggi non si governa" [Today one does not govern against the Fascists]. Such efforts are sometimes perceived as dangerous by the disloyal opposition when it considers the partner capable of reasserting authority, as was the case with Giolitti in Italy. In Germany we have the tentative attempts of Brüning and Schleicher, and finally the "successful" cooptation of Hitler by von Papen that made the Führer chancellor and master of Germany.

In such attempts at cooptation it is characteristic of the disloyal opposition to bargain initially for only a limited share in power, perhaps a few ministries; but as the regime parties withdraw from a position of strength and resistance to its claims, the disloyal opposition increases its demands. In the case of the "March on Rome" the demands escalated from some cabinet seats to the premiership. We should not forget that the Fascists in the first Mussolini cabinet had only six of the sixteen portfolios, or that Hitler and the other three Nazi cabinet members were "flanked" by eight conservatives in addition to von Papen as vice-chancellor. The nature of the portfolios claimed is also significant: If those in control of the police and armed forces (and today, the mass media) are transferred to the opposition, any defense of democracy becomes impossible. On the other hand, as Salandra notes in his memoirs about negotiations with Mussolini, when the opposition controls the viol streets and its leader does not enter the government, the entry into the cabine ministers and the exclusion of the ministry of interior would leave the government position. De Felice, *Mussolini il fascista*, vol. 1, p. 346.

31. This is a central theme in Sartori "European Political Parties," pp. 137–76, which contains his analysis of the dynamics of such party systems. The analysis is confirmed by electoral returns in Germany after 1928, in Austria and Spain in 1936, and in Italy since 1948. (However, some observers want to read the Italian returns differently, considering not the parties but the distance between parties—concretely, the growing PCI—and the Center in terms of ideology, policy actions, and the perceptions of the electorate.)

32. In May 1936 the Rex party had polled 11.5 percent of the vote, and its leader, aroused by mass rallies, sought a plesbiscitarian election in Brussels by ordering one of the Rexist deputies to resign. This forced a by-election. The democratic parties—Catholics, Liberals, and Socialists—realizing that their division might prove fatal, agreed on a single candidate: the prime minister. The vote would be thus for or against the regime. Everyone, including the Cardinal-Archbishop of Malines, mobilized to condemn the movement. The 19 April 1937 poll totaled 175,000 for Van Zeeland, and 69,000 for Degrelle, including the votes of the Flemish Nationalist UNV. Rex did not recover from the defeat produced by the unity of the democratic parties.

33. The Facta government, welcomed by the Fascists for its weakness, blocking other alternatives, is a prime example. Facta himself had little desire to assume the burdens of office and considered himself a stand-in for Giolitti, who was waiting for the right moment to return to power. Schleicher and von Papen before the Machtergreifung were also leaders of this sort, as were several of the prime ministers and ministers imposed by Alcalá Zamora between 1933 and 1936 and Casares Quiroga Azaña's prime minister after his elevation to the presidency of the Spanish Republic.

34. Building on a complex tradition in constitutional theorizing (linked mainly with the name of Benjamin Constant) Carl Schmitt in his influential *Der Hüter der Verfassung* (Tübingen: J. C. B. Mohr [Paul Siebeck], 1931) developed the idea of *neutrale Gewalt* [neutral power], and its "independence" from the pluralistic party-state (pp. 132–59). See also his "Das Zeitalter der Neutralisierungen und Entpolitisierungen" (October 1929), reprinted in *Positionen und Begriffe in Kampf mit Weimar-Genf-Versailles: 1923–1939* (Hamburg: Hanseatische Verlagsanstalt, 1940), pp. 120–32, and "Übersicht über die verschiedenen Bedeutungen und Funktionen des Begriffes der innerpolitischen Neutralität des Staates" (1931), in the same volume, pp. 158–161.

35. Tönu Parming, *The Collapse of Liberal Democracy and the Rise of Authoritarianism in Estonia*, Contemporary Political Sociology Series, no. 06-010 (Beverly Hills, Ca.: Sage, 1975); Georg von Rauch, "Zur Krise des Parlamentarismus in Estland und Lettland in den 30er Jahren," in *Krise des Parlamentarismus in Ostmitteleuropa zwischen den beiden Welkriegen*, ed. Hans-Erich Volkmann (Marburg/Lahn: J. G. Herder Institut, 1967), pp. 135–55; and Jürgen von Hehn, *Lettland zwischen Demokratie und Diktatur*, Jahrbücher für die Geschichte Osteuropas, Supplement 3 (Munich: Isar Verlag, 1957). For a history of these short-lived, smaller European democracies, see Georg von Rauch, *The Baltic States: The Years of Independence. Estonia, Latvia, Lithuania, 1917–1940* (London: C. Hurst, 1974).

36. One of the signs of crisis of a regime and ultimately one of the contributing factors in its breakdown is the tendency of the military leadership to take an "attentist" position, to identify itself publicly with the "State" or the "nation," and to avoid committing itself to the regime. This was the position of von Seeckt and many high-ranking Spanish office's', including Franco. It allowed them not to confront their more politicized colleagues, with whom they did not fully disagree, and to attempt to maintain a semblance of unity in the armed forces under the cloak of neutrality. Such a position eventually became untenable, and younger officers increasingly felt that in a polarized society they had to take sides. An army like the Italian, which, confronted with the Fascist assault on power, "would do its duty but would prefer not to have to do it," obviously limits the decision-making capacity of the political leadership when it is confronted with political violence. Certainly no regime can allow officers or even ex-officers to have any relationship whatsoever with political paramilitary groups. (For bibliographic references, see other chapters in this volume.)

CHAPTER 4

1. See, for example, Jules Moch, "De Gaulle d'hier à demain," *La Nef* 19 (July–August 1958):9–15. Remembering his role as minister of the interior in May 1958, he writes of "The Fear . . . that on account of the balance of forces and their dynamics, the disorders, if they should explode, would benefit the Communists exclusively. Prague in 1948 haunted my sleepless nights as much as Madrid in 1936." Guy Mollet came back to the same theme, in *13 mai 1958–13 mai 1962* (Paris: Plan, 1962), pp. 11–13, when he argued in favor of de Gaulle, saying: "The government of colonels would have come to power almost without 'coup ferir'. I know that possibly one or two thousand courageous men would have been sent to slaughter, but that would have been the Spanish [Civil] War without the republican army. In that hypothesis, I believed that it [the government of colonels] would have lasted twenty or thirty years." Here Guy Mollet perceives, with brilliant insight, the sad fact that breaks with democratic legitimacy are not easily reversed.
2. See Lepsius, "Machtübernahme und Machtübergabe: Zur Strategie des Regimewechsels."
3. This sense of urgency is reflected in Mussolini's expression "O ora o mai piú" [Either now or never]. Once this stage of serious negotiations for cooptation is reached, the leaders of the antisystem forces also start feeling an urgency to attain power, and to fail to do so is risky for them. Recriminations among leaders about a willingness to sell out for a "minister's seat" might split the party between revolutionaries and pragmatists; the masses, now mobilized for action, might not be available on another occasion; the opportunistic supporters (particularly financial backers) might feel that the movement is a "bad investment," since it does not have the drive to power; and the regime-supporting forces might regain confidence and unite.

   In spite of his negotiations with Giolitti, Mussolini said: "It is necessary to put the masses into action, to create an extraparliamentary crisis and to get into the government. It is necessary to prevent Giolitti from getting into the government. As he has fired against D'Annunzio, he would give the order to fire against the fascists." De Felice, *Mussolini il fascista*, vol 1, pp. 304–5. It was at that point that Pareto, in a letter to Pantaleoni, perceived the danger of "domestication" of Fascism by the "fox," Giolitti, and he and leading Fascists felt the urgency of "revolution" before abandoning the drive and losing their following. Ibid., p. 304. The texts quoted by De Felice, and many analyses of the time, illustrate that even at the eleventh hour a "real statesman" with authority over the army and the civil service who is "willing to shoot" can be a threat to the breakdown or overthrow of democracy.
4. An opposition confident of its chance to seize power will devote considerable attention to establishing contacts and using a mixture of reassurances and more-or-less veiled threats to neutralize the opposition of institutions like the churches (in the case of the Catholic countries, the Vatican), business groups, Freemasonry, the monarchy, even the trade unions, and to encourage them to withdraw their support from the political parties of the democratic regime. In some cases this involves the manipulation of factional cleavages within those institutions. This is also true for those aiming to displace an authoritarian regime in crisis, as any reader of the statements of the Spanish Communist party today would know.

   In *Mussolini il fascista* De Felice gives evidence of the increasing intensity of such moves by Mussolini between the Naples party congress and the March on Rome.
5. There are numerous examples, but let us mention a few. In Italy, the Catholic church, particularly the Vatican, foreseeing the prospect of a Mussolini government started having secret contacts with him. What is more important, the church began withdrawing its identification with the Popolari party, particularly by disapproving of clerical activity in politics. This undermined Sturzo's position. In Germany, the relationship between the Zentrum party, the church, and the Vatican at the time of the Nazi *Machtergreifung* has been the object of scholarly polemic. The debate has centered around the contributions of Rudolf Morsey ("Die deutsche Zentrumspartei," in *Das Ende der Partein 1933*, ed. Erich Matthias and Rudolf Morsey), and Ernst-Wolfgang Böckenförde ("Der deutsche Katholizismus im Jahre 1933," in Gotthard Jasper, *Von Weimar zu Hitler, 1930–1933* [Cologne: Kiepenheuer and Witsch, 1968], pp. 317–43; and "Das Ende der Zentrumspartei und die Problematik des politischen Katholizismus in Deutschland," ibid., pp. 344–76). A similar Vatican policy has

been noted in Ricardo de la Cierva, *Historia de la Guerra Civil Española* (Madrid: San Martín, 1969), pp. 478–79, in relation to the Republic shortly before its advent in 1931. Even the trade unions, so closely tied to the Socialists and other radical parties, sometimes begin following a strategy separate from that of the parties, become available for semiauthoritarian alternatives, affirm their own identities, and, as the policies of D'Aragona and Leipart after the Fascist and Nazi takeovers show, hope to survive under the new regime.

In Italy, the CGL (Confederazione Generale del Lavoro) showed an increasing tendency to act independently of the Socialist party, particularly at the time of the "pacification pact." On 6 October 1922, before Mussolini became prime minister, it had already denounced its pact with the Socialist party to "maintain itself free from any ties with whatever political party, considering such an act indispensable to maintain the trade union unity." This policy was encouraged by Mussolini and continued until the Matteoti murder with renewed vigor. See De Felice, *Mussolini il fascista*, vol. 1, pp. 380–85, 598–618.

On the growing distance between the positions of trade unions and the Social Democratic party in Germany, see Erich Matthias, "Der Untergang der Sozialdemokratie 1933," in Jasper, *Von Weimar zu Hitler, 1930–1933*, pp. 298–301, and Karl Dietrich Bracher, Wolfgang Sauer, and Gerhard Schulz, *Die Nationalsozialistische Machtergreifung: Studien zur Errichtung des totalitären Herrschaftssystems in Deutschland 1933–1934* (Cologne: Westdeutscher Verlag, 1960), pp. 175–86. The German developments in 1933 are all the more surprising in view of the Italian experience.

Business interests are even more cautious in relation to an opposition that might take over a regime. They are ready to include such parties among those receiving a share (whose size depends on the party's prospects and "reasonableness") of their contributions, in order at least to maintain access to party leadership, if not to influence or shape policy. Sometimes the social position of leading businessmen allows them to act as go-betweens in the "politics of the small c's," often in the interest of the "pacification" so important for business.

6. Adolf Hitler, in his famous "oath of legality" at the Leipzig Reichswehr trial in 1930, when he spoke with impunity before the court. Quoted in Bracher, *Path to Dictatorship, 1918–1933*, p. 117.

7. Laski, *Democracy in Crisis*, passim.

8. Editorial in *El Socialista*, 16 August 1933, quoted in Stanley G. Payne, *The Spanish Revolution: A Study of the Social and Political Tensions That Culminated in the Civil War in Spain* (New York: Norton, 1970), pp. 108–9. For other expressions of the same thought, see pp. 108, 111, 137. Largo Caballero, leader of the maximalist wing of the PSOE and ex-cabinet member, put it in these terms just before the 1933 election:

> I say to you that if we win on the 19th we shall make the capitalists change their minds. But if we lose, it seems to me that we will enter a new period in which electoral activity will not be enough. It will be necessary to do something more powerful—anything but renounce our ideals. There will be no justice so long as socialism does not triumph. Only when we can hoist the red flag of revolution on the official buildings and towers of Spain will there be justice.

For a further discussion of the tragic conflict in the Spanish Socialist party, see my chapter on Spain in this volume.

9. This is not the place for an analysis of the Fascist phenomenon and its role in the interwar crisis in Europe. For references to the constantly growing literature see Laqueur, *A Reader's Guide to Fascism*. In that volume the reader will find also our own definition of Fascism and an analysis of its appeal and of the social bases of Fascist movements (pp. 3–121).

10. Theodore Draper, "The Ghost of Social Fascism," *Commentary*, February 1969, pp. 29–42. See also Weber, *Die Wandlung des deutschen Kommunismus*, vol. 1, pp. 232–47.

11. Even in more solidly established regimes than France in 1958, we would not expect a distribution of responses different from that shown in the table on p. 122.

12. From that perspective, the history of the Weimar Republic from its birth to the late twenties offers interesting examples: the Kapp Putsch, the Beer Hall Putsch, and the attempts made by leftist extremists. We might also mention the February 1934 crisis in Paris, when the Leagues threatened Parliament, and the May 1968 threat to the Gaullist Fifth Republic. On the latter, see Bernard E. Brown, *Protest in Paris: Anatomy of a Revolt* (Morristown, N.J.:

Response to Questions: What Would You Do in the Case of a Communist Uprising? In the Case of a Military Uprising?

Military Uprising	Communist Uprising				
	Support the Regime	Do Nothing	Support Uprising	No Answer	Total
Support the regime	4.6%	1.4%	2.4%	0.5%	8.9%
Do nothing	11.0	59.2	2.4	1.6	74.2
Support uprising	3.0	2.2	0.5	0.1	5.8
No answer	0.8	0.8	0.3	9.3	11.2
Total	19.4	63.6	5.6	11.5	100.1 (2624)

For a detailed analysis, see Cohn, "Losses of Legitimacy and the Breakdown of Democratic Regimes."

General Learning Press, 1974); and Philippe Benéton and Jean Touchard, "Les interprétations de la crise de mai-juin 1968," *Revue Française de Science Politique* 20, no. 3 (June 1970), 503–44.

The case of Finland is particularly interesting, since the dangers of extreme multipartism, the presence of the third-largest Communist party in the West, and its proximity to the USSR would have made the stability of its democracy dubious. See Kevin Devlin, "Finland in 1948: The Lesson of a Crisis," in Hammond and Farrell, *Anatomy of Communist Takeovers*; and C. Jay Smith, "Soviet Russia and the Red Revolution of 1918 in Finland," idem, pp. 71–93.

Another interesting case in which conditions for a stable democracy seemed absent but a regime managed to consolidate itself is studied in Frank Munger, *The Legitimacy of Opposition: The Change of Government in Ireland in 1932*, Contemporary Political Sociology series, vol. 2 (Beverly Hills, Ca.: Sage, 1975).

CHAPTER 5

1. The idea of treating a social system as a "state of equilibrium" was one of the contributions of Vilfredo Pareto. See *The Mind and Society*, 122–25, and esp. chap. 12, numbers 2060–70 ff. It was further developed by L. J. Henderson, and through his teaching and the work of Parsons it has entered the mainstream of sociology. Let us quote Pareto's formulation: "We can take advantage of the peculiarity in the social system to define the state we choose to consider and which for the moment we will indicate by the letter X. We can then say that we state X is such a state that if it is artificially subjected to some modification different from the modification it undergoes normally, a reaction at once takes place tending to restore it to its real, its normal, state" (2068). In Pareto's view all states of equilibrium have such a dynamic aspect, are not inherently incompatible with change ("progress"), and are obviously not always desirable or valuable from everyone's perspective. All "states" of a social (or political) system in a Paretian view are in a constant process of adjustment. Here we are dealing with those situations—to which he refers in his discussion—in which there is not merely a small, continuous, imperceptible alteration of the system, but a major disruption after which elements in the system are capable of responding without changing some of their basic relationships (in this case, democratic institutions) and reaching a new stable situation.

2. An important source for understanding the unique role of de Gaulle in French politics is Institut Français d'Opinion Publique, *Les français et de Gaulle*, with an Introduction by Jean Charlot (Paris: Plon, 1971), which brings together the survey data on the general from 1945

until after his death. Innumerable tables give evidence of the charisma that surrounded him at many points in his career and of the retrospective approval of his role as a statesman. On the response of politicians to him at the time of the 1962 election, see Mattei Dogan, "Le personnel politique et la personnalité charismatique," *Revue Française de Sociologie* 6 (1965):305–24, and the essays on de Gaulle in Stanley Hoffman, *Decline or Renewal: France Since the 1930s* (New York: Viking, 1974), pt. 3.

3. Hirschman, *Exit, Voice, and Loyalty,* p. 24.

4. See Max Weber's discussion of "objective possibility" in "Critical Studies in the Logic of the Cultural Sciences: A Critique of Eduard Meyer's Methodological Views," in *The Methodology of the Social Sciences,* trans. and ed. E. A. Shils and H. A. Finch (New York: Free Press, 1949), pp. 113–88; see esp. pp. 180–85.

5. There is a basic difference between the return to democracy after German occupation, particularly when exiled governments insured the continuous legitimacy of institutions, and return to democracy after the establishment of nondemocratic regimes—in Italy, Germany, Austria, Japan, and even Vichy France, for example. It should not be forgotten that in the latter cases democracy was only reestablished by the victors. (See Robert A. Dahl, "Governments and Political Oppositions," in Greenstein and Polsby, *Handbook of Political Science*, vol. 3, pp. 115–74, esp. pp. 155–58.) In addition, in those cases nondemocratic rule had not lasted long: seventeen years in Italy (1926–45), twelve in Germany, eleven in Austria, and eight in Japan. This alone should differentiate those cases from that of Portugal, in which democracy was restored after forty-eight years, and Spain, in which the process took thirty-seven. In Portugal, it was the military, after colonial defeat, rather than internal pressures, that overthrew the authoritarian regime, and the reestablishment of competitive democracy is still seriously in doubt. Of the overthrown democracies, only Greece and some Latin American countries (Venezuela, Colombia, Argentina, Brazil, and Chile) have returned to more or less unstable democratic rule as a result of internal developments after periods of authoritarian rule. Gianfranco Pasquino, in "L'Instaurazione di regimi democràtici in Grècia e Portogallo," *Il Mulino* 238 (March–April 1975):217–37, underlines the difference in duration of those two regimes in accounting for the different outcomes.

6. Robert A. Kann, *The Problem of Restoration: A Study in Comparative Political History* (Berkeley and Los Angeles: University of California Press, 1968).

7. Terry Nardin, *Violence and the State: A Critique of Empirical Theory* (Beverly Hills, Ca.: Sage, 1971).

8. This is the classic distinction of the scholastic political theorists between legitimacy of origin or title and of exercise. While democratically legitimate in origin—that is, freely elected—such governments exercise their power in ways contradictory to the values underlying democratic politics.

9. This point is emphasized in Bendix, *Max Weber,* p. 300, and in Johannes Winckelmann, *Legitimität und Legalität in Max Webers Herrschaftssoziologie* (Tübingen: J. C. B. Mohr, 1952).

10. Alexis de Tocqueville, *Democracy in America* (London: Oxford University Press, 1946), chap. 34, pp. 583–84.

11. Joseph A. Schumpeter, *Capitalism, Socialism, and Democracy* (New York: Harper and Brothers, 1950), pp. 291–93, emphasized, as a second condition for the success of democracy, that "the effective range of political decision should not be extended too far." In fact, Schumpeter noted "democracy does not require that every function of the State be subject to its political method."

12. Merkl, *Political Violence under the Swastika.*

13. Karl Loewenstein, "Legislative Control of Political Extremism in European Democracies," pp. 591–622 and pp. 725–74, is an excellent review of those efforts.

14. Clinton L. Rossiter, *Constitutional Dictatorship: Crisis Government in the Modern Democracies* (Princeton, N.J.: Princeton University Press, 1948), is a detailed analysis of the functions and dangers of emergency rule in democracies, including the multiple uses of Article 48 of the Weimar Constitution and French, British, and American laws and practices. A final section, setting up eleven criteria of *constitutional* dictatorship, is particularly interesting in connection with the problem of reequilibration of democracy (pp. 297–306).

15. Pareto, *Mind and Society,* number 2186.

16. See the influential formulation by Herbert Marcuse, "Repressive Tolerance," in *Critique of Pure Tolerance* (Boston: Beacon Press, 1965). For a critique, see Alastair MacIntyre, *Herbert Marcuse: An Exposition and a Polemic* (New York: Viking, 1970).
17. Sartori, *Democratic Theory*, chap. 16, pp. 418–19 and 444–45.
18. *State and Revolution*, quoted in ibid., pp. 421–22.
19. Rosa Luxemburg, in her essay "The Russian Revolution," written in prison (1917–1918). That essay is included in *Rosa Luxemburg Speaks*, ed. Mary-Alice Waters (New York: Pathfinder, 1970), pp. 365–95; see esp. p. 394.
20. Ibid., pp. 389–90.
21. We do not enter into the question of "how" democratic those regimes, which according to our definition can be considered democratic, actually are. We enter even less into the somewhat different problem of how far "social" and "economic" democracy has been achieved in the "political" democracies. Indeed, political democracies differ in their "democraticness," and there have been attempts to measure that degree. For an interesting discussion, see May, *Of the Conditions and Measures of Democracy*.
22. This was, let us remember, the Communist position when the theory of social-fascism was formulated, at the time the Nazi flood was rising. The KPD (Kommunistische Partei Deutschlands), in a resolution by its Central Committee in May 1931, declared: "The fascist dictatorship does not in any way represent a contrast in principle to bourgeois democracy under which the dictatorship of the finance capital is also carried out. [It is] simply a change in the forms, an organic transition." In February 1932 the committee noted that "democracy and fascist dictatorship are only two forms that harbor the same class content.... They approach each other in their external methods as well...." The practical implications of this ideological position were formulated by a KPD parlamentarian as follows: "When the fascists come to power, then the united front of the proletariat will come into being and sweep everything away. To starve under Brüning is not better than under Hitler. We are not afraid of the fascists. They will mismanage faster than any other government." Quoted by Richard Hamilton in a forthcoming book on the social bases of Nazism.

Index

Abel, Theodor, 94
Accountability, elections and, 19
Acton, Lord, 117 n. 22
Allende, Salvador, 71, 73
Antidemocratic: ideology in Germany, 9; mass movement and civil war, 84; perceptions of reform parties, 34; reaction of privileged, 4
Argentina, 72; post-Perón democracy in, 35
Armed forces, 59, 60, 73, 76, 85; authenticity and, 70; legitimacy and, 17; loyal opposition and, 36, 37; loyalty "test" and, 30; as minority, 85; revolution and, 15. *See also* Army; Military, the
Army, 59, 83; Italian, 119 n. 36; legitimacy and, 30; Soviet, 15. *See also* Armed forces
Austria, 7, 43, 59, 65, 76, 90
Authenticity, abdication of, 69–71
Authoritarian regimes, 70, 77, 79, 97; breakdown and, 6–7; founding democracy after, 34–35; restoration after, 92; unsolvable problems and, 51
Authority, 11, 70, 102 n. 29, 105 n. 7; force and, 16, 17, 23; goals of, 19; political force and, 58–59; Rose's analysis of, 37; violence and, 15

Barnard, Chester I., 106 n. 18
Bavaria, 59, 65
Belgium, 25, 67
Bell, Daniel, 78
Borders: defining, 46–47; paramilitary groups and, 59
Bracher, Karl Dietrich, 4, 39, 99 n. 3
Brazil, 73
Breakdown of regimes: action preceding, 39; authoritarian, 7; cabinet instability and, 110–12 n. 44; cause of, 93; conspiracy theory of, 78; defined as competitive democracies, 5–8; effectiveness and, 22–23; efficacy and, 18–22; elements of, 14–49; explanation of, by social scientists, 4; exter-

nal intervention and model of, 68–69; leader's awareness of, 99 n. 5; legal revolution and, 76–80; legitimacy and, 16–18; loss of power and, 75–77; military leadership and, 119 n. 36; model of, 4–13, 99 n. 4; multiparty systems and, 27; oppositions and, 29–38; patterns of, 80–86; precipitation of, 54, 55; process of, 50–75; reequilibration after, 87–92; revolution and, 14–16; semiloyalty and, 33; unsolvable problems and, 54; violence and, 14–15, 56–58
Breitscheid, Rudolf, 99 n. 5

Calhoun, John C., 85
Capitalism, 47; crisis and, 38
Catholic church, 29; Mussolini and, 120 n. 5; natural law tradition and, 102 n. 30
Catholic political participation, 45, 47, 53
Chile, 14, 71, 73
Civil liberties, 6; loyalty "test" and, 30–31; radical critics' arguments concerning, 95; violence and, 57
Civil war, 76, 84; in Spain, 84–85
Class, crisis strata and, 56. *See also* Masses
Clausewitz, Karl von, 52
Coalitions, 65–67, 69; 75; legal revolution and, 77
Collectivity, 19–20
Colombia, 90
Communism, 47
Communists, 15, 59, 72, 79, 92, 96; in France, 88–89; interpretation of Fascism by, 84–85, 124 n. 22; Italian perception of, 110 n. 40; loyalty and, 29; in Spain, 84–85
"Consociational democracy," 8
Constitution: armed forces as defenders of, 73; new democracies and, 40–41; reform parties and, 34; in Spain, 35; Weimar, 70
Constitutional monarchies, 9
Coopting, 66, 75, 77–78, 79, 118 n. 30, 120 n. 3

125

...t is legit. If mili perceives that
the pop. doubts efficacy of regime → breakdown
...personal security, civic order, predictability in
...ating decisions.